TRIATHLON
The Skills of the Game

TRIATHLON

The Skills of the Game

STEVE TREW

THE CROWOOD PRESS

First published in 1989 by
The Crowood Press
Ramsbury, Marlborough,
Wiltshire SN8 2HE

British Library Cataloguing in Publication Data

Trew, Steve
  Triathlon, the skills of the game
  1. Triathlon
  I. Title
  796

  ISBN 1–85223-188-2

Acknowledgements

I should like to extend my thanks to Great Britain swimming coach, Maurice
Sly, not only for welcome help and advice, but also for his coaching all
those years ago! In addition, thanks are due to the following: Norman
Brook, national athletics coach for Northern Ireland; athletics coach,
Malcolm Blackmore; physiotherapist, Mike Varney; Dave Scott, who made
such an impression as a triathlete – and as a human being; John Day, of
Day's Cycles, and bike mechanic Mark Trent; Le Coq Sportif clothing and
Arena swimwear, especially Janie Hazlewood; Biddie Foord of Terrapin
Wetsuits; Andy Widgery, Great Britain team manager, and Dick Poole,
chairman of the BTA; all the triathletes from whom I have learnt so much,
and my wife, Veronica, who – with the exception of the press picture of
Dave Scott – took all the photographs in the book and supplied the
encouragement to keep me going.
All line drawings except Fig 71 by Vanetta Joffe

Typeset by Chippendale Type, Otley, West Yorkshire
Printed in Great Britain at The Bath Press

Contents

Having been a competitive cyclist for over thirty years, I never dreamed that I would ever change my sporting interests – but I did! I got involved and then thoroughly 'hooked' on triathlon from its very beginnings in Great Britain.

My interest began because of my coaching qualification in cycling, seeing my first triathlon and realising that the majority of the participants obviously knew very little about cycling! In those days, most of the competitors were only average performers in one of the three disciplines, and had little idea how to put together a programme of training – furthermore, as it was such a new sport, there was no one to ask and no literature to be found.

Fortunately all that has now changed, and a great deal of the knowledge gained during the past few years has been embodied in the following pages to enable the beginner to make a much better informed start in this fascinating sport than his or her predecessors. Go for it, and have fun!

Dick Poole
BTA Chairman 1983–1989

This was the book I might have written . . . but I was relegated to telling you how wonderful it is and how everyone should rush out and buy it . . . and indeed you should!

Steve Trew is one of the original tri-fanatics who has carried his tremendous enthusiasm and national level athletics experience to all departments of our sport, from journalism to international competition and now to coaching. He has helped me on many occasions, both with my own training projects and in providing a sympathetic ear and a friendly word of advice in my times of need, but there are also many others who have benefited from his Mediterranean training camps and the encouragement meted out so generously to all and sundry.

Steve Trew's love affair with triathlon has been carried forward into these pages. They will undoubtedly provide a considerable amount of information to enable all triathletes, but in particular the beginners, to wade through the triathlon paraphernalia and vocabulary, to fix their perspective and to settle into the triathlon habit with much enjoyment for years to come.

Sarah Springman
British Champion

I met Steve Trew in the summer of 1984 soon after he had successfully finished a race. His friendly encouragement and enthusiasm for triathlon impressed me so much that I began competing myself a few weeks later. I was hooked immediately.

It has been my privilege to work alongside Steve with the national team who are the rising force in Europe, and his understanding of athletes of all standards and the requirements of the sport are second to none.

This book, based on practical racing experience, will undoubtedly provide the beginner with a marvellous start and the already initiated with substantial suggestions for improvement.

Andrew Widgery
Great Britain Team Manager

Introduction

ONCE UPON A TIME . . .

Triathlon history dates back to around 1974 in Southern California when a group of friends began to get together to work out in training. The group contained mostly runners, a few swimmers and the odd cyclist or two. It wasn't long before the group was organising informal fun runs and races, followed by races containing swimming and running, and a natural progression led them to include cycling. They decided to call this amalgamation of three disciplines, Triathlon.

At the beginning it made no impact on the general non-sporting population at all, nor, at that time, did any of these athletes think that it ever would. However, the word did start to spread a little, and gradually other triathlons began to be organised up and down the Southern California coast, many around the San Diego area. Many of these were on a very informal basis with would-be competitors having to ask around to discover where the next event would take place. The reason for this of course, was that the same people who organised these fledgling events were also the ones who wanted to win them! Other modified triathlons and quadrathlons began to take a hold on those athletes who were becoming a little jaded with single sport competition and canoeing was sometimes included, or sometimes the run was split into two or more parts. Some races were relays and some were events where teams of two had to complete the course together; perhaps a two-man canoe would be used. Some of these early races are still going strong fourteen years later.

HAWAII

One of the group of friends who started competing in the multi-sport events in California was a Navy Captain, (now Commander) John Collins. In 1977, the year he turned forty, he competed in the around-Hawaii relay race, a running event. After the race, as often happens, the beer began to flow, and, endurance events often favouring older competitors, Collins came up with a proposal for a new race.

There were three tough races on the Hawaiian island of Oahu at that time: the Waikiki rough water swim of 2·4 miles; the around-the-island bike race of 112 miles which was held over two days; and the Honolulu marathon over the classic distance of 26·2 miles. John Collins proposed that they be combined into an 'Ironman' race. Although many laughed at him, the idea wouldn't go away, and on 18 February 1978, it became reality when fifteen athletes lined up on Waikiki beach for the first ever Ironman race. The winner was Gordon Haller in a time of 11 hours and 46 minutes. Twelve of the fifteen starters finished the course.

Gradually the race grew. In 1980 Dave Scott – 'Mr Ironman' – won for the first time from a field of 108 starters, breaking the course record by almost two hours. The 1980 race was filmed for American television and by 1982 it was becoming big

Fig 1   Dave Scott.

business. Oahu became unable to host the race as the numbers of athletes who wanted to compete grew from the initial fifteen to over a thousand. So the Ironman race was moved to the island of Hawaii itself, the media remained interested and ABC TV deemed it one of their most popular coverages. In 1982 the drama of the television coverage was to ensure that triathlon became known to all. Julie Moss was leading the women's race but, within sight of the finish line, she collapsed and began to crawl agonisingly towards the tape with the eyes of the American public watching her and sharing in her torment. There was no happy ending for Julie as Kathleen McCartney ran past her to finish first. Triathlon's success was guaranteed by media coverage.

Media coverage has also ensured that Dave Scott is the best-known triathlete in the United States, if not the world. Dave Scott had won the Ironman *six* times by the summer of 1988. He was the first to beat ten hours, the first to beat nine hours, and in 1986 became the first to finish in under eight and a half hours. His fellow competitors call him 'God' and they're only half joking. Dave's perennial rival in the Ironman race is another Scott, Scott Tinley. Tinley has won the race twice and has also finished in second and third place. He is one of the very few triathletes who are capable of racing Ironman distance races and taking part in other triathlons at the highest level throughout the racing season. Tinley and Scott make up half the group known as the 'big four'. The other two are also Americans, Mark Allen the five-time winner of the Nice World Championships and Scott Molina – 'the terminator'. These four *do* get beaten, but only infrequently, and usually by each other.

However as the sport progresses more and more triathletes try to usurp the old guard but their early introduction to the sport will hold them in good stead as the young pretenders attempt to challenge them.

FROM NEW WORLD TO OLD

Triathlon started in California, it grew in media terms in Hawaii, and in 1982 it came to Europe.

American superstar triathlete, Scott Tinley was charged by IMG with organising a triathlon in the principality of Monaco after a previous ambitious plan to involve France, Italy and Monaco had to be abandoned for logistical reasons. The organisation for the race had already gone ahead when the death of Princess Grace of Monaco forced it to be abandoned and the pre-planning and arrangements were moved to Nice.

Another American superstar, Mark Allen, won that first race and successfully defended his title another four times before deciding to forgo the 1988 race in order to try to beat Dave Scott in the Hawaii Ironman.

GREAT BRITAIN

Another competitor who didn't attract quite so much attention was an Englishman, a newsagent named Aleck Hunter. Aleck was to bring the sport of triathlon to Great Britain. He was enthralled by the race, amazed at the level of fitness of the top Americans who dominated that first race, and determined that one day British triathletes would reach the heights that the Americans had. But as we know, the stronger the base, the higher the pinnacle of success. Within months of returning home to Dagenham in London, Aleck had

Introduction

Fig 2 Aleck Hunter, the man responsible for the initial growth of triathlon in Great Britain, changes a tyre.

Fig 3 Aleck Hunter in cycling action.

got together with Olympic pentathlete Mike Ellis and cyclist Dick Poole, a former holder of the John o'Groats to Land's End long distance cycling record. In the saloon bar of a pub in Hammersmith, the British Triathlon Association was formed and in a short time, Britain has achieved international recognition in the triathlon world. Our two best-known triathletes who have gained European and World honours are women who coincidentally both share the same Christian name.

Both Ladies, Both Sarahs

Sarah Springman has won two European championships at the Ironman distances, and finished in the top five at both the recognised World championships at Nice and Hawaii in 1985, when the two races were held only two weeks apart! (Imagine doing a double marathon race, and then fourteen days later, taking on a triple marathon – that, in triathlon terms, is what Sarah Springman did.)

Sarah Coope has won three European championships at the half-Ironman distance, and in 1987 achieved a magnificent treble by winning all three European championships at sprint distance in Marseilles, half-Ironman distance in Roth, Germany and at the Ironman distance in Finland. She has also finished second in the Nice World Championships in 1986 after a fantastic running section which saw her move up from fourteenth place along its twenty mile stretch eventually finishing third only to be promoted to runner-up spot when first

Fig 4   Sarah Springman, the best known triathlete in Great Britain.

Fig 5   Sarah Coope, holder of many European titles.

5

placer, Erin Baker of New Zealand, was disqualified for receiving water outside the official drink stations.

And the British Men

Several British athletes were involved in the early days of international triathlon competition at Nice, Steve Russell and Mike Harris finishing twelfth and thirteenth with only the top American pros ahead of them in 1983. There was no recognition of triathlon feats in the British press at that time and the two men's achievements went largely unnoticed, except by other like-minded

endurance athletes who were fired with enthusiasm by their success and no unnaturally, set out to try to emulate them Mike Harris is still competing and stil winning many major British races. Britain's first male European champion was Glenn Cook who won the half Ironman title at Roth in 1987. Glenn won the first London triathlon in 1984 and gradually increased his training and knowledge of the sport so tha he is now acknowledged and respected as one of the best in the world. Glenn was also one of the first British based triathletes to take the chance of going to America to live and train throughout the winter, and learn

Fig 6   Mike Harris and Steve Russell in training.

wherever he competes. Even in the highly competitive professional circuit in America he has been able to beat the Americans at their own game. The trend set by Sarahs Coope and Springman and Barel and Cook will continue and triathlon will become more and more a universal sport with rising standards as athletes train scientifically with an increasing knowledge of the demands of the sport.

Fig 7   Steve Russell, twelfth in Nice in 1983.

rom the originators. Many others now ollow him.

THE FUTURE

he gap between the big four men in America and the rest of the triathlon world s closing, with not only other Americans chasing them but also other Europeans at ast beginning to make an impact. Holland, or example, is a nation with a strong riathlon reputation. A favourite is Rob Barel, a triathlete who commands respect

Fig 8   Rob Barel, top European triathlete, pictured with Belgium's Lieve Paulus after the European short-course championships in 1986.

1 Getting Started

The primary aim of any first time triathlete, just like any first time marathon runner, is to cover the distance and finish. If the triathlete achieves that, he has won the battle over himself and the aching muscles which have been begging him or her to stop and rest.

The athlete who is well prepared in training may be tempted to stop but will carry on anyway, knowing that the satisfaction of finishing will be reward enough and that to give in would be to betray the time and the miles spent in swimming, cycling and running, indeed, almost a cheating of oneself. The first aim in training then is to cover the distance.

There are triathlons of all distances raced in Great Britain, even including an Ironman event in Peterborough in 1985. Many triathlons are based around swimming pools or sports centres and have the swim inside. Because of the number of competitors and the restraints of having to swim in lanes and going off at staggered times, these races tend to be the shortest, often with a swim distance of only 4 or 600m. To keep the cycle and running legs on a par with this, they are also shortened. However after this entry level triathlon, there are races where the distances are becoming, to a certain extent, standardised.

These distances are those which are rapidly becoming accepted as the standard 'short' distance triathlon and are used for the Great Britain championships and the American and European circuit of races. The distances are as follows:

1,500m swim (110yds short of a mile)
40km cycle (25 miles)
10km run (6¼ miles)

Each of these distances would be a formidable challenge in itself to the unfit novice, but challenges are what triathlon is all about. There are literally thousands of triathletes covering these distances in a competition every summer weekend in Great Britain, and almost all of these will have doubted their ability to complete a race when the thought of triathlon first entered their minds.

Fig 9   Ricky Morris covers the distance.

Figs 10–12   *Many smaller, local triathlons take place in swimming pools.*

Fig 11

Fig 12

But they do complete the race. And then they talk about it and laugh about it with their friends and rivals, and discuss how they can go faster next weekend.

COVERING THE DISTANCE IN TRAINING

The real secret of triathlon, to enjoy the race and compete well, is that it is essential to be properly prepared in training. For the novice or first timer, being properly prepared means first having covered at least the racing distance in training, and then covering it many times.

Getting Started

Are you fit enough to start training? No one expects you to start as a Dave Scott or a Sarah Springman, but you do need to ensure that you are medically able to embark upon a training schedule, particularly if you are overweight, have not taken part in physical activity for a long period of time, or are past the first flush of youth. A visit to your doctor is not only advisable, but plain common sense, as you are about to start on a road which may well change your lifestyle both for the good and for ever. Make sure you're fit enough to begin.

Gently does it

When the running boom hit America, and then crossed the Atlantic, in the early seventies, jointly fuelled by the American Frank Shorter's marathon victory at the Munich Olympics and a greater public awareness of fitness and health, many good athletes destroyed their chances of fulfilling their potential by starting training at a pace and intensity that meant they would almost certainly break down with injuries. The marathon distance of 26.2 miles became the race to run with the more sensible challenges of a 10km or half marathon largely ignored in the enthusiastic but perhaps misplaced euphoria of taking on the distance which had the mystical reputation of being the man-killer.

The first golden rule is to *make haste slowly*. Start to train gently and easily, giving your body a chance to recover between sessions. By doing triathlon training, you already have an advantage over single sports exponents; because you're working out in three different sports you are using different muscle groups so the likelihood of stiffness, soreness, or overuse injury is that much less.

So, if you've decided to give it a try, how do you get going and what do you look out for?

First of all, choose an event to enter and to prepare for. Make it for the coming season, but make it far enough ahead to give yourself a reasonable chance of going into it well-prepared. Then sample the atmosphere of an event by going along to see a triathlon race if you haven't done so already. By doing this you will make a self-commitment to take part in the future. Everyone looks at competitors in races or fun runs and thinks, 'If he can do it, then so can I'.

Get Set

Next comes the tough bit. You have to take a long, critical look at yourself and decide

Fig 13   Triathletes mass on the edge for a lake swim.

upon your strengths and weaknesses in all three disciplines.

Building up distance and stamina is the most important thing at first.

SWIMMING

If you're not a swimmer, then swimming should be the initial starting place.

A competent swimmer will finish a triathlon even if the bike ride consists of easy pedalling and coasting downhill, and the run is a mixture of jogging and walking. A poor swimmer may not even complete that first discipline, so you need to have the confidence in yourself to be able to finish a mile swim.

Swimming is the most technically demanding of the three sports and along with building your stamina and competence to cover distance, it is more than

worthwhile to have your swimming stroke checked out by someone who knows what to look for. Unfortunately, adult swimming classes are few and far between and usually have a long waiting list. Clubs for the competitive swimmer are geared towards 11 (or younger) to 20 year olds and do not cater for the adult learner, although some have a social section where swimmers' parents can get in the water. Do be persistent in seeking advice as it's very difficult to judge how good your own stroke is and the time spent in finding someone who can be an objective observer will not be wasted.

When you are happy that your technique is at least reasonable, set yourself an acceptable challenge, such as eight lengths of the pool without stopping. Work on that until it's easy, then build up by adding another couple of lengths and then another couple. It shouldn't be too long

Fig 14   A river swim section means that triathletes have to tread water before the start.

before you're able to do a quarter of a mile without stopping, and then half a mile. With the knowledge that you're gradually coming to terms with the distance, now's the time to start worrying about increased speed. Start to intersperse one fast length every three or four easy ones, then make it two fast ones each time and you'll soon be getting there! An added side bonus when you start to put in some faster work will be that sessions begin to go so much more quickly as the variations in speed take away any boredom that may have been creeping in.

Your confidence will be enhanced with good comfortable equipment so invest in a nylon or lycra swimsuit and a pair of goggles. There is other equipment which can make a difference in the early days while you're striving to build up confidence and also improve technique and add strength. A kickboard is made of expanded polystyrene or similar and is held in front of you with arms extended, hands gripping the edges while your legs and feet kick the water behind you. A pull-buoy is shaped to fit between your thighs and will keep your legs horizontal without having to kick, allowing you to concentrate on your arm stroke. Fins or flippers can also be used to develop the leg kick, and while these can give a false sense of speed, they are invaluable in helping the very poor kicker who has trouble maintaining his legs in a horizontal position even when kicking, and also add some strength.

Open Water

An event with a massed start in a lake or the sea is vastly different from the heated pool where you can cruise comfortably up and down a lane with an eye on the line painted on the bottom of the pool. In an open water

Fig 15   Anxious moments before the flag goes down.

Fig 16   A sea swim can mean horrendous waves and conditions, even
making it difficult to get into the water.

Fig 17   A massed start swim looks and feels like being in a washing-
machine!

start you'll be poked, kicked and splashed and you will swim more slowly, so plan accordingly. A rule of thumb used by many triathletes is to add on about ten per cent of their pool times to judge their estimated finishing times for an open water event. An additional factor is the cold so do try to get some open water practice in before you race. Under no circumstances should you swim alone, but go along with a friend, preferably one who can row a boat along-side you, keep near the shore, and make sure that someone knows where you are. The cold water can cause problems for the unprepared triathlete, and the first immersion can be a most unpleasant experience, taking your breath away and giving rise to feelings of panic. It's important to stay rational and relax and your body will gradually acclimatise to the temperature. Most triathletes wear two rubber swimming hats and some will wear a neoprene hat in the same material as a wetsuit to keep body heat in during races, knowing that as much as a third is lost through the head. Gradually working up to longer and longer periods spent in cold water is the only sensible way to progress.

CYCLING

Everyone has ridden a bike at some time in their lives. Most people who ride regularly backwards and forwards to work feel competent to control their machines, even in heavy traffic and the secret of confidence on the bike is just that, to ride regularly. The cycling section of a triathlon is the longest both in terms of time and distance, and in the early days of training and competing the biggest and quickest improvements can be made on this discipline. Over the standard 40km distance an improvement

from 24 to 25km per hour will save about 6 minutes, although as speeds improve the amount of time saved will become progressively less.

Cycling novices will need to concentrate on handling the bike and on being able to pedal efficiently. As with swimming, any advice that can be gained from more experienced cyclists should be eagerly sought. An increase in covering the distance should be matched with a gain in technique, which will be achieved more easily – and perhaps only – if the bike fits. As you gradually step up the mileage and spend more time in the saddle, comfort will become a very important factor. Professional cyclists are concerned with their position on the bike to the point of obsession – Tour de France riders have even been seen adjusting their saddle height while the race is in progress as any mechanical alteration which will save them physical effort is worthwhile.

The bicycle is the single most expensive purchase that you will make as a triathlete and it is important to buy the right one. Of course, you may be training or competing on a borrowed or second-hand bike at the start, but considerable adjustments can be made to the riding position as long as the frame size is reasonably suitable. Along with the frame size, the most important considerations are the top tube length, the seat height, the handlebars and the handlebar stem.

Frame Size and the Top Tube

Most people will find that a mass-produced frame from one of the big bicycle manufacturers will fit them. Reputable bike shops will be prepared to help and give advice on what to look for. There should be around 5cm (2in) between the top tube and your

Fig 18   The large fields mean that triathletes are often closely bunched together. They must avoid drafting on the bike section or run the risk of disqualification.

Fig 19   Robin Brew is accompanied by TV cameras during a European
championship race.

rotch when you stand astride the bike. When you sit in a stable position on the saddle, it should be possible to straighten the leg out completely on the downstroke.

In the last few years, the wind trainer has become an increasingly common piece of training equipment for cyclists. It is very handy to be able to make use of this when checking out your bike as you can be closely observed and instant feedback can be obtained as to the suitability of your riding position. It is then easy to make immediate adjustments.

The length of the top tube should allow you to stretch comfortably although not so much that you transfer your body weight over the handlebars and fatigue your upper arms and triceps. Triathletes with a swimming background, where they have built up their upper bodies, should exercise particular caution when tempted to opt for a longer top tube.

Seat Height

As with swimming and running, it must be remembered that triathlon cycling has certain different demands from pure cycling. The demands of running, particularly on the athlete, mean that the seat height needs to be adjusted slightly higher than for pure cyclists. A higher saddle will give more power on the downward push when the leg is fully stretched out; this will lead to less pressure on the powerful gluteal muscles which in turn will prevent some of the anticipated discomfort of the running section. Also, the upper quadriceps (at the front of the thighs) take less stress with a higher saddle, allowing a fuller and more comfortable stretching out of the legs during the earlier part of the run.

When you are sitting correctly on the saddle, your leg should be almost com-

pletely straightened when your foot is at the bottom of the pedal stroke. A final pushing and straightening out of the knee will take the heel of the foot to fractionally below the pedal. If you are wearing cycling shoes with cleated soles, it is important to take this into account when determining riding height.

Handlebars and Handlebar Stem

Triathletes may wish to use a wider set of bars than the conventional 40cm measurement, especially those with a swimming background who have powerful, wide upper bodies. The slightly wider and less aerodynamic riding position is more than compensated for by being able to breathe more easily. The correct length of the stem can best be judged by placing your hands on the drop section of the bars and looking directly downwards; if you are staring directly over the stem and feel comfortable, the position is correct. The stem is normally about level with the saddle height.

Riding Position

The best position for cycling is one that is aerodynamic, allows you to ride efficiently, and keeps your body as relaxed as possible with the back in a curved position, removing the strain from the shoulders. As the miles build up and the triathlete gains more experience, he or she will be able to experiment with the body position, perhaps trading off comfort against speed and learning how to move position without dropping speed too much. As with swimming and running, more time spent in the practice of the activity will lead to better results. A more detailed look at riding position will follow in the chapter on cycling.

Getting Started

Fig 20 Dave Candy shows good aerodynamic, yet relaxed, form.

RUNNING

Introduce yourself to running in much the same way as with swimming and cycling. Start easily, gradually increase the distance, then add a bit more. Force yourself down to the local running track – you'll be surprised at the different standards of runner and jogger that are down there and how easy it is to be invited to go out on a run, whatever your standard. *Don't*, however, try to do too much too soon. It's easy to spot the cyclist or swimmer who has been carried away by doing too many miles. The legs go wooden, refuse to bend and stairs become a major hazard to overcome. A general rule of thumb would be to increase the mileage by no more than ten per cent each month; this may not seem

much but it will build you up from 30km (2 miles) to 60km (40 miles) a week in ju seven months. When you have built up a endurance running base – and, if you ha a swimming or cycling background, you' already well on the way – it will be time move up to a little speed. Start alternatir fast and slow stretches, perhaps usir lampposts as a guide for distance, striding up each hill that you come to.

If you haven't done so by now, do g along to the local running or jogging clu as having other runners around you is great help for pace judgement.

As with swimming, do get decent equi ment. Essential for running is a pair quality training shoes with sufficient paddi and good support to make the hurti tolerable. Ultra-light racing shoes can b

nsidered when you have decided to
ove up a step from active participation.

HANGING OVER

ansitions are a shock to the system. The
st, from swimming to cycling is reason-
ole; you're transferring much of the effort
om the upper body to the legs. The real
oblem comes on the cycle/run change-
er. A lovely mistranslation from Japanese
Is it thus, 'The willing I had, the able I was
ot'. You just have to practise it in training
get used to it in races. Your legs must
djust from being used in one way to being
oused and misused in another. They feel
ead and rubbery. Your feet feel as though

js 21–22 *The transition areas are a focal point for
triathlons and are usually crowded. To
avoid the crowds, get out of the water
or off your bike in first position!*

they have a small block of wood beneath
each sole after pressing hard on the pedals
for so long. Your legs will feel better as you
keep running, but it can take as long as a
quarter of an hour for the discomfort to
disappear.

RACEDAY

This is what you've planned and trained for
over the last few months, so don't let
yourself down by poor preparation now.

1. Leave plenty of time for everything;
work backwards from the race start time
and plan accordingly.
2. Check and double check your kit.
There's nothing worse than being up for a
race and then finding that your running
shoes are at home in a different bag! You
will need: entry number and race information; running shoes; vest and shorts; hat
and sunglasses; swimsuit; swimcap and
swim goggles; a wetsuit if it's an outdoor
swim; bicycle; helmet; cycle shoes; cycle
shorts; cycle top; or a trisuit if you wish to
dispense with the three sets of individual
clothes; your bike (do the mechanical
checking before you arrive at the race);
pump; spare tubs (tubular tyres); socks;
towel; cycle mitts; a reasonable amount of
bike tools; elastoplasts; watch and a change
of clothing for afterwards.
3. Arrive early and check in at race
registration, ask if there are any changes to
the published race programme.
4. Make sure that you know the course.
5. Set out your clothing and bike equipment in a logical order in the transition area.
6. Make sure you know the entrance and
exit for the transition area.
7. Be at the start in plenty of time.
8. Stay calm.

Fig 22

Fig 23 Time is saved in transition by struggling out of your wetsuit on the way out of the water.

Figs 24–25 Careful preparation and setting out of clothing and equipment in the transition area can save valuable time.

Fig 25

24

Fig 26   Patrick Barnes at over 70 years demonstrates that triathlon really is
for everyone.

THE TRIATHLETE

So, you can cycle, you can swim, you can run. Careful, you're on your way to becoming a triathlete and your life may never be the same again!

What does triathlon offer to the athlete who wants to compete, to enjoy him or herself, to train at a reasonable level, and to race without ever necessarily dedicating his life to the sport?

It offers a chance of 'all round fitness' without the risk of the overuse injuries that can be associated with running, or indeed any single sport when carried out to excess. The carry over of fitness, particularly cardiovascular endurance, is considerable. Triathletes even have a word for it, 'crosstraining'. The chance of boredom or disillusionment

is almost non-existent. If you are fed up wit the jarring and pounding on your legs, giv running a miss for a couple of days and d a little more swimming. Sprained wrist Sore shoulder? Leave the pool alone an go for a spin on your bike. The combina tions are endless.

A word of warning, though. Just becaus you're fit in one sport, able to finish a 65kr (10 mile) cycle ride or a half marathon rur it doesn't automatically follow that you'r going to be able to leap into triathlon an transfer your fitness directly. Different mus cles are used for the different activities and, when the same muscles are brougt into play, they're used in different ways The delicious agony when you jump off you bike after a 50km (30 mile) ride, feeling O and then discovering that your legs hav

Fig 27   Super veteran Patrick again in the midst of anxious triathletes waiting for the start.

Fig 28   Triathlon is an individual endurance event. Any mishaps or
mechanical failures have to be dealt with by the athlete.

Fig 29 Finishing makes it all worthwhile, in whatever position.

completely disowned you for the running section, is something to be experienced. Nothing will prepare you for it that first time, although you will be able to laugh about it afterwards when you've discovered the delights of back-to-back training.

Think back to the days when you first started in your own individual sport – you probably took it a lot easier than you do now. Gradually getting more involved, gradually training harder and seeking out new challenges until you arrived at fitness.

Well, that's just how you have to take on the triathlon, building up gradually.

IS IT FOR YOU?

Before shying away from even the idea or entering or training for a triathlon, remember that on a fitness and health level nothing could be better for you. You will avoid any muscle overuse injuries, you will be exercising extensively aerobically ensuring a strong heart and more endurance than you will know what to do with.

On a competitive level you will be breaking out of the rut, meeting not only a new challenge but also new people from a variety of sporting backgrounds.

The camaraderie of triathletes is something to be experienced – the common sharing of an experience that is still wrongly viewed as 'over the top' tends to bring everybody together.

ESSENTIALS FOR STARTING OUT ON TRIATHLON

1. Choose an event and enter it. You have an aim to go for.
2. Listen and take advice from others but be selective.
3. Never attempt to rush your training in the beginning; make haste slowly.
4. Join the British Triathlon Association. You'll get help, advice and information, and a full fixture list plus insurance.

2 Swimming

The swimming section of a triathlon differs in one very important respect from any other swimming race; the competitor has to emerge from the water with sufficient energy to first cycle, and then to run for a considerable time. Therefore it is important that the athlete covers the swim as smoothly and in a manner as energy saving as possible, without going into oxygen debt. The differences between the expert swimmer and the novice swimmer are perhaps more marked than between the expert and novice cyclist and runner; and although the

swim is the shortest section of the triathlon in terms of both distance and time, massive gains can be made on this discipline with an efficient and energy saving stroke.

THE FRONTCRAWL

The fastest and most efficient stroke is the frontcrawl. When done correctly, it is the most streamlined and the most powerful. The arms tend to dominate the stroke, and the arm movement to a large degree is

Fig 30　The clothing and equipment for swimming.

29

natural, i.e., the muscles are used in a manner which provides the strongest action, and the crawl allows the most profitable application of force as far as the laws of motion are concerned. Although some triathletes do swim either breast-stroke or backstroke in races, they are rarely to the front of the field and the extra effort involved in attempting to stay level with the frontcrawlers does little for their chances in the remaining two disciplines. In examining the stroke it is important to look at five areas.

1. *Body position.*
2. *Leg action.* Although the leg action is not the main propulsive force, it does ensure that the body is held in a good swimming position.
3. *Arm action.* The arms are the main source of propulsion.
4. *Breathing.* An economical breathing technique which does not interfere with the stroke is essential for full development for both speed and stamina.
5. *Timing.* The co-ordination of the previous four areas combine to form the overall complete stroke.

Body Position

Moving through and overcoming the resistance of the water is the first principle of swimming and therefore the more flat and streamlined the body, the better. The head and shoulders, hips and legs will be in a straight line, a further indication that the frontcrawl is technically superior to other strokes.

The rolling of the body as an aid to the turning of the head required to breathe in frontcrawl in no way takes anything away from this, as, seen from the front, the same mass is presented to the water whether parallel to the surface or at an angle to it. In any case the amount of body roll will be

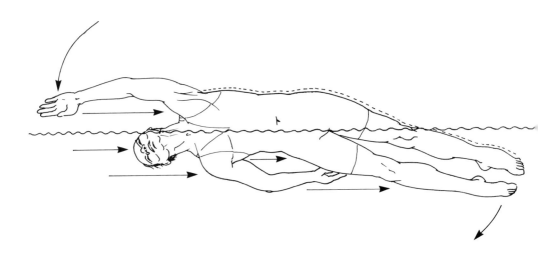

Fig 31   As the arm swings out wide on recovery, the leg reacts in an equal and opposite way by moving to the side, so distorting the body from its straight line.

governed by individual flexibility; those who are less mobile in the neck and shoulder areas will need to roll more in order to maintain an efficient stroke than those who are supple in these areas.

Distortion of the straight line from head to toe will occur when any body part moves too far to the side. The head may lift and turn a fraction too far or the arm action, either on propulsion or recovery, may move too far wide of the shoulders and pull sideways and back, causing the lower leg to move towards the hands and the hips to move away, creating an unwanted and noticeable sideways zigzagging effect.

Commonwealth and Olympic swimming coach Maurice Sly summarises the body position thus:

1. Relatively flat and streamlined when viewed from the side and top.
2. When viewed from head on, a limited amount of rolling about the longitudinal axis is allowed.
3. The carriage of the head governs the body position. It can be used to adjust the position of the shoulders, hips, legs and feet.
4. The shoulders should be as high as personal buoyancy allows but not higher than the head. Novice swimmers tend to bury the head.
5. Stable hips are a sign of good technique. The hips should roll at the same time as the shoulders, so flexibility of the spine is essential.

It is important to remember that many triathletes will wish to wear wetsuits to counter the cold, and extra buoyancy will be provided by the neoprene rubber with resulting adjustment to the body position.

Fig 32   Wetsuits are almost essential wear for our cold water . . .

Leg Action

The powerful muscles grouped around the hips are used to initiate the leg kick which is then taken over by the leg muscles themselves. This creates an overall action of a slow starting movement becoming an accelerating whiplash type of wave as the power moves down the leg.

With most open water swims being between 1,000 and 1,500m, it is important that triathletes don't overkick in an effort to gain speed, but concentrate on a steadying two beat kick to maintain a good, flat, aerodynamic position counterbalancing the arms. The two beat kick may appear slow and uncomfortable to start with, but it does minimise the use of energy, an important factor which will pay dividends later in the course of the race. Many triathletes with

Swimming

Fig 33   . . . while some triathletes prefer to go without.

a swimming background will be used to a six beat leg kick and will feel comfortable maintaining this in triathlon races. However, the sport is triathlon, not swimming, and even good swimmers may wish to debate the advisability of a six beat kick in their metamorphosis to triathlete. It is worth experimenting with the two beat kick, and then if it doesn't feel comfortable, remain with the six beat kick. Triathletes don't just have to be good swimmers, they have to take the legs as prime movers into the next two disciplines where they need to be fresh, not tired from overkicking.

Maurice Sly summarises:

1.   The kick starts at the hips and travels through the knees to the toes.
2.   The kick should be within the body width, the legs passing up and down close together in a loose relaxed manner.
3.   The ankles are stretched for stream-lining.
4.   There is a slight intoeing of the feet.
5.   The depth of the kick should be between 30 and 45cm (12 and 18in).
6.   The 'normal' kick has very little bending at the knees (like a flexible fishing rod which enables the rolling action of the body to be integrated.
7.   The flutter kick has considerable increase in the knee bend which enables a rearward thrust to be made, helping the forward drive.
8.   The two beat kick, 'left arm right leg' 'right arm left leg', is the natural kick for distance swimmers, whereas the six beat is more standard for sprint swimmers.
9.   The crossover kick is due mainly to excessive rolling thereby appearing to give an odd number of kicks per arm cycle.

Many triathletes coming into the sport from a non-swimming background — cycling particularly — have very little ankle flexibility after years of specific training where good plantarflexion (pointing the foot and toes downward to the floor) is not required, and experience a lot of difficulty in overcoming problems created by a poor kicking action. The realisation that this is a triathlon race and not a swimming race should put this problem into perspective, but if the kick is so bad that it is a real hindrance, it would be helpful to spend some time on ankle flexibility and good plantarflexion. As with everything in triathlon, the gains and losses must be put into the perspective of the time spent.

Arm Action

The arm action can be looked at in five phases, although there are no distinct dividing lines and the stroke is a continuous movement.

Entry

The hand enters the water in front of the swimmer between lines projected forward from the centre of the body and the shoulder. Too wide an entry creates unwanted resistance.

Some swimmers will stretch forward above the water before placing the hand in, while others will enter just a little in front of the head and then slide forward under the surface.

It is important that the elbow is higher than the hand upon entry, for without this high elbow position a good underwater arm action is unlikely. As the hand breaks into the surface the fingertips enter first with the outside of the hand pushed slightly upwards. This helps to keep the elbow high and avoids too much splashing. If the elbow is *not* higher than the hand on entry, it will dip into the water first or the entire arm will drop creating extra work for the swimmer to put the hand in the correct position before the catch and pull phase can take place.

Maurice Sly summarises:

1. The arm entry should be clean and neat with minimum splash.
2. The entry should be made in front of the leading shoulder, between the centre line of the head and the shoulder line.
3. A normal entry is made with the finger tips first, although in some cases swimmers with limited flexibility will enter with the thumb first.
4. The entry point should be made with the wrist and elbows flexed, not limp.

Fig 34   The entry. Note the elbow higher than the hand to facilitate both a smooth entry and to prepare for a good underwater arm action.

Swimming

Fig 35 The catch. The hand has moved downwards and is now just a
hand's depth below the water surface, ready to start the pull phase.

5. The elbows at entry will be higher than the wrist which will be higher than the hand.
6. A swimmer's physique will normally determine the reach and position of entry.

Catch

The catch position is the starting point for the backward pull of the hand and arm and is about the depth of the hand beneath the water surface. The wrist bends towards the inside of the forearm in order to shape the hand to press on the water.

Maurice Sly summarises:

1. The position where the hand gains purchase of the water is normally between 10 and 15cm (4 and 6in) below the surface.
2. The aim must be to maintain that purchase throughout the pull.
3. To obtain and maintain maximum purchase, the hand is shaped and pitched.
4. The elbow is higher than the wrist which is higher than the hand.

Pull

The hand presses downwards at the start of this phase and as the elbow starts to bend, the hand is pulled backwards and under the body. Many non-competitive swimmers attempt to pull with the elbow unbent and the arm almost straight, but it can be seen that by doing this the hand first travels downwards, then backwards and

finally upwards in a semicircular motion – the reaction of the body is to push it upwards, then forwards and downwards.

The maximum elbow bend will occur when the shoulder, elbow and hands are level, just after the hand has passed under the chin.

Weak swimmers will find it a temptation to allow the elbow to lead the hand which will result in a poor pull with the hand being allowed to slip through the water as the elbow pulls it backwards. To correct this, overcompensate by trying to fix the elbow still and bend the lower arm only until it is level.

Maurice Sly writes:

1. The pull starts at the catch position.
2. The hand accelerates due to the bending of the elbow.
3. The pull is via a series of variable length levers from long to short; the shortest lever used is with an elbow bend of up to 90 degrees.
4. A high elbow, wrist and hand position is maintained throughout the pull.
5. The arm bends to maintain maximum pressure from which there should be no release.
6. Strength, flexibility and technique govern the bending of the arm.
7. The hand moves backwards under the face and the chest.

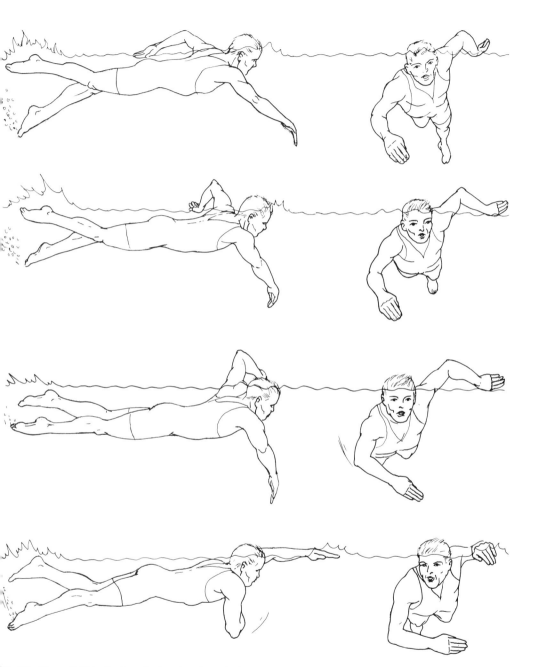

Fig 36 The pull. This displays the hand and arm in the pull phase. The
hand presses downwards and the elbow starts to bend (a), the
hand is then pulled backwards and under the body (b and c) until
maximum elbow bend is reached (d) with shoulder, elbow and
hand level, just fractionally past the chin.

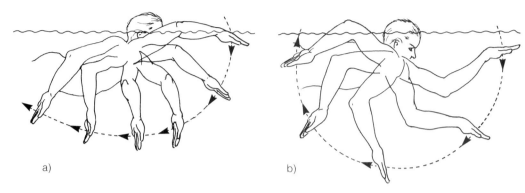

a)

b)

Fig 37 Weak swimmers may allow the elbow to lead the hand (a), rather than the hand leading the elbow (b).

Push

The push phase takes the hand past the chin, straightening out the arm until the hand exits from the water past the hips. This is the part of the arm action which should generate the most power and is the most important phase for gaining speed; many poor swimmers gain little forward thrust from this phase with the hand moving backwards only a little and coming out of the water level, or even in front of the waist.

The stronger swimmer will continuously and powerfully straighten the elbow and bend the wrist upwards so that the maximum area of the palm of the hand is still pushing backwards. The push phase continues to take the hand underneath the body until it finally moves outwards to clear the body before breaking the water surface. To practise the push phase in the initial learning stages, triathletes may wish to almost fully extend the arm and see how far below the hips they can touch their leg with the thumb. In any case the longer stroke is important for the triathlete who is trying to maximise energy saving on this discipline.

Maurice Sly summarises:

1. The push is the second half of the underwater propulsive phase.

2. The push takes over from the pull underneath the body past the hips to the thighs.
3. The whole of the surface of the inner arm should be exposed to apply pressure and therefore aid propulsion.
4. The acceleration of the hand is maintained.
5. The push should pass the hips to the thighs to almost full arm extension before releasing the pressure.
6. As the hands approach the thighs, they start to round outwards to miss the body.
7. The pitch of the hands varies throughout the arm action to maximise the pull and push.

Recovery

The recovery phase takes over as soon as the push has finished. It starts even before the hand has cleared the water, as the elbow finishes straightening out. The body roll is towards the other, underwater arm and this, combined with the elbow flexion serves to release the arm and shoulder from the water.

After release from the water, the elbow bends and brings the recovering arm forward ready to start the whole cycle again. The amount of elbow bend and therefore the height of the recovery varies tremendously

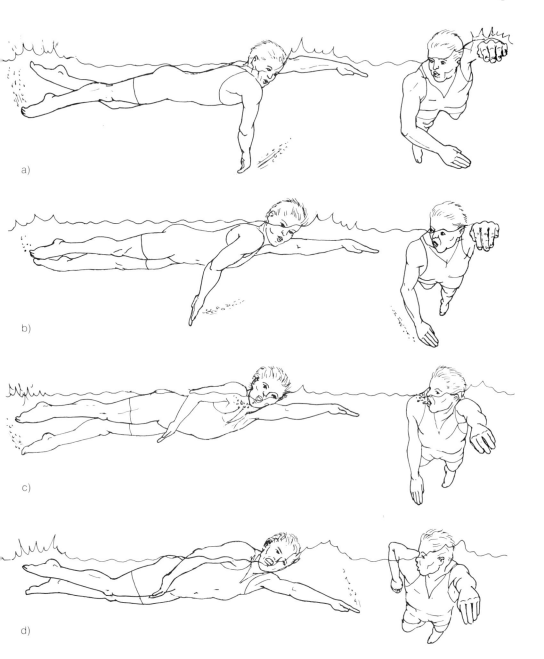

a)

b)

c)

d)

Fig 38   The push phase. The hand continues to travel past the chin (a),
gradually straightening out and generating power (b, c and d) until
it is ready and in a position to begin the recovery phase. Note the
hand past the hips (d), having travelled backwards a long way and
ensured maximum forward thrust.

Swimming

Fig 39   *The recovery has already started with the hand still in the water (a),*
and continues with the elbow bending and bringing the arm
forward (b) to start the whole cycle again (c).

with those from a swimming background tending towards a high recovery while those who are not – and this will include the majority of triathletes – and who have less mobile shoulders, have a flatter recovery with the arms swinging outwards in a semi half-circling movement. This is commonly known as the ballistic recovery. There are many recovery actions between these two extremes with some swimmers having an asymmetric action with one arm lifting high and the other swinging out wide.

An exaggerated sideways recovery can create problems with the straight body line being forced out of alignment to compensate for the wide recovery.

Maurice Sly writes:

1. Recovery starts at the release of the hand pressure.
2. The elbow leaves the water first, bringing the relaxed lower arm close to the body.
3. With the elbow high, minimum use of energy is employed as the recovery should be a rest phase.
4. Fluency of movement is essential.
5. If the recovery is rushed, the rhythm of the stroke is destroyed.
6. In the recovery, the shoulder mobility governs the limb track.
7. During the first part of the recovery, the palm faces back.
8. Towards the end of the recovery, the palm faces the water.

Breathing

Breathing in swimming should interfere with the stroke as little as possible. However, for triathletes with a non-swimming background it is the breathing which can create fear and hinder improvement. Panicking to get enough breath and then panicking further on having to place the face downwards into the water to exhale is not conducive to the slow, deep, relaxed breathing which is required for triathlon.

Triathletes should breathe on each stroke cycle (every two strokes); one full action of left and right arms. Sprint swimmers who breathe every four or six strokes are not concerned with conserving energy

Fig 40 A fast start is essential to get away from the milling masses. Some swimmers here even overtake the starter's boat.

and are soon into oxygen debt which must be avoided in triathlon swimming. For those who breathe naturally to the right, the breath is taken as the left arm is in the catch position and the right arm in the press phase (and vice versa for those who breathe to the left). With the head turned to the side, the breath is inhaled and the head is rotated so that the face is back in the water for the swimmer to exhale.

There is no need for the triathlete to lift the head as the breath is taken because the speed of swimming generates a bow wave just in front of the swimmer's head with a trough created behind it, and it is in this trough that the head turns to the side and the breath is inhaled.

Maurice Sly writes:

1. To breathe, the head is turned in time with the shoulder to the chosen side until the mouth just clears the water surface.
2. Breathing takes place when the leading hand is at the catch position and the other is just finishing the push.
3. The head should be centralised after inhalation.
4. The mouth should be shaped to breathe in the bow wave below the normal surface of the water.
5. The swimmer should wait until the opposite hand enters the water before turning the head to breathe.
6. The head travels with the body roll, but slightly further.

Fig 41   If you're in with the wrong speed swimmers, it can be unpleasant, uncomfortable and even quite scary.

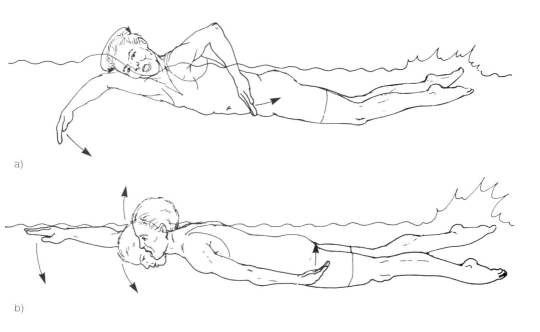

a)

b)

Fig 42   The swimmer normally breathes to the side in the trough of the bow
wave created by swimming forward at speed (a). When lifting the
head to sight in open-water swimming (b), the breath should still be
taken to the side and the head then rotated forward. Lifting the head
directly will tend to make the swimmer push downwards, so taking
the body out of alignment.

7.   Breathe looking sideways and forwards, or sideways and backwards.
3.   A minimal, non-hindering breathing
action should be the aim.

For open water swimming, triathletes will
need to lift their heads to sight on an object
and check their course. The breath should
still be taken to the side and the head then
rotated forward to check that they're head-
ng in the right direction. The head should
not be held in this high position as this will
nevitably push the body and feet down,
creating a drag effect. A further compli-
cation is that triathletes will need to breathe
to both sides from time to time to check
their position on the course and their close-
ness to other competitors. This bilateral

breathing will usually feel unnatural to
begin with but the time taken to learn the
skill is well spent as it gives an immediate
awareness of position in the race. It can be
practised in the swimming pool by breathing
every three strokes or by breathing on the
'wrong' side for alternate lengths. Occasional
wrong side breathing during a long swim
will also help to dispel any tightness in your
neck and shoulders.

Timing

Timing of the frontcrawl stroke depends
upon how well co-ordinated the arm and
leg actions and the breathing pattern are.
   The smoothness of an experienced
swimmer contrasts vividly with the jerky,

uncoordinated action of the novice who seems to put in twice as much energy and take twice as many strokes to swim twice as slowly as his more experienced counterpart. Swimming is the most complex skill of the three disciplines and time spent on the basic strokework will not be wasted.

Maurice Sly writes:

1. Overall rhythm of constant movement is essential.
2. Timing in frontcrawl swimming can vary from six beat in sprinting, i.e. six leg kicks to one arm circle, to four beat and two beat even number plus crossover.
3. A flash of the palm of the hand and the sole of the opposite foot denotes correct timing and good co-ordination.

4. Swimmers can and often do change timing by switching from one leg kick to another.

This section on swimming has, of necessity, concentrated on the frontcrawl as it is the stroke that will be used in races. However, as the triathlete improves and grows in confidence, he or she will want to experiment and try out the other strokes breaststroke, backstroke and butterfly. Not only will this add to the 'feel' for the water and a greater awareness of what is happening during all phases of the stroke, but it will also give a greater enjoyment of swimming for its own sake and an incentive to make use of these new skills during training sessions.

Fig 43   Cold water takes its toll. The triathlete here grabs a hot drink before getting on to his bike.

3 Cycling

Pure cycle racing on the road can be divided into roadracing *per se*, where all the competitors start together with the first across the finishing line the winner, and time-trialling where the competitors start at intervals, usually a minute, and the fastest cyclist over the distance is the winner.

Roadracing can be extremely tactical with teams protecting the team leader from the brunt of the hard work and trying to man-oeuvre their sprinters into a good position for the explosive effort at the end. Races of over a hundred miles will often be decided by the thickness of a tyre. It is an exciting event both for the competitors and for the spectators who watch their favourites jostling for positions.

Time-trialling is the classic situation of one athlete against himself and the stop-watch. It requires a constant effort of solitary riding without any respite or protec-tion by team-mates, the only other human company being when you overtake or are overtaken by a rival. It means unrelenting, self-inflicted pressure. In France, where cycling is more a religion than a sport, the time-trial is called 'the race of truth'.

The cycle section of a triathlon, where

Fig 44   The cycling section is an individual time-trial.

Cycling

Fig 45   The riders here spread over the road to avoid drafting.

drafting and packriding is forbidden, is a time-trial.

THE BICYCLE

In Chapter 1 'Getting Started', reference was made to the importance of the correct equipment. In particular, the bicycle is the single most expensive purchase that a triathlete will need to make. It is crucial that the bicycle fits the rider, and not a case of the rider being made to fit the bicycle. Many, even most, triathletes will start their triathlon career on a borrowed bike. This is sensible, for an early retirement from the sport would mean money wasted on valuable equipment. However, once the decision is made to compete regularly in triathlon,

expert advice should be sought on getting the right bike. For discussion on correct frame size, top tube, seat height, handlebars and handlebar stem, *see* Chapter 1 'Getting Started'.

Every triathlete's and cyclist's position on the bike is unique to the individual; mimicking the style of a favourite hero may be satisfying to the ego but it is unlikely to give an automatically good riding position. The ideal is to provide the athlete with a position which gives maximum efficiency with every effort, and an even weight distribution over the three contact points between body and bike.

An efficient riding position will be one that is relaxed, yet aerodynamic. The wind resistance encountered on a bike will be quite surprising to the triathlete who comes

Fig 46   The bicycle.

Fig 47   The low body position ensures less wind resistance.

into the sport with a running background. The running speed is relatively low when compared to cycling speed and any wind encountered while running is not usually remarked upon unless it is exceptionally strong. The more quickly the rider cycles, the more progressively strong the wind resistance becomes. The novice cyclist should experiment by freewheeling down a long hill, first in a completely upright position and then in a full aerodynamic position with the upper body pressed close to the top tube when the increase in speed and acceleration will be significant.

Hand and Arm Position

The hands should be relaxed on the bars but gripping hard enough to give control. It is aerodynamically better to ride with the hands on the drops although this may feel uncomfortable for the newcomer for any length of time, and it may feel preferable to ride with the hands on the brake hoods even though this is usually in a less aerodynamic position. However, the effects of wind resistance can be reduced in this position by the triathlete bending his arms to 90 degrees at the elbows and riding with the arms parallel to the top tube.

When climbing hills, riders will usually move their hands to the top of the bars, which helps to break the monotony of a single held position and also helps alleviate some stiffness. A tightness may be felt at the top of the shoulders by the neck after having had to hold the head up when riding with hands on the drops, and bending the

Fig 48   This triathlete has his arms too straight and body position too upright.

Fig 49   Ricky Morris shows a good low position.

head momentarily to look down at the top tube may remove some stress, but at all times, you must, of course, look where you are going.

Feet and Leg Position

As soon as triathletes get to grips with cycling, they will want to buy cleated shoes which have shoeplates to slot into the pedal and give maximum leverage on the upstroke as well as on the downstroke. Before doing this, novice cyclists will have discovered a line forming along the bottom of the shoes they have been using for cycling, put there by the metal ridge along the back of the pedal. When fitting cleats to

the bottom of shoes, it is well to use the experience gained here and fit the cleats so that the pedal groove will exactly match the line already there. The ball of the foot should press more or less directly down over the pedal spindle, so you do not have to point your toe too much at the bottom of the pedal stroke if, for example, the foot is too far forward on the pedal, which can cause cramping in the arch of the foot. Also, avoid having to push too hard at the top of the pedal stroke which can occur if the foot is too far back on the pedal.

An incorrect foot position can cause pressure on the knee and fatigue in the quadriceps.

Fig 50   Hands are on the drops for an efficient aerodynamic position.

Fig 51   Hands on the brake hoods for more comfort.

Fig 52   The 90° position, hands on the brake hoods but still
aerodynamically efficient.

Fig 53   Hands on top of the bars, often used for climbing. This is
comfortable for easy riding but can make it difficult to react and
grab the brakes in an emergency.

Fig 54   Note the slightly pointed foot position at the top of the pedal stroke.

Pedalling

Thoughts on pedalling speed divide into two camps: those who advocate fast pedalling with a low gear (up to 120 pedal revolutions per minute), commonly called 'spinning' or 'twiddling'; and those who advocate slower pedalling with a high gear (as few as 60 pedal revolutions per minute), commonly called 'pushing'. Triathletes should try out all speeds of pedalling and decide which suits them best, remembering always that the race does not end with the cycle section but that there is a run to follow. Individual comfort is paramount with the triathlete being able to go into the run in a not too fatigued state. Overuse of either pushing or spinning can be detrimental and the triathlete should aim for something in between, perhaps around 90 revolutions per minute with a gear appropriate to this.

The temptation for novice cyclists is to concentrate on the downward stroke to the exclusion of everything else. This is to be avoided and the triathlete should aim for a smooth pedalling action which not only takes into account the downward push, but also emphasises the upward stroke and an awareness of a circular action. Time spent on this circular motion will ensure that the pedalling action smooths out and is not just a series of interconnected jerking movements.

The foot should be fairly flat at the top of the pedal stroke and remain flat or pointing slightly downwards as you initiate the ownward and forward action. At the beginning of the upward and backward ction, the heel will lift slightly to add omentum to the movement. The feet can et cramped if they are fixed into the edals too tightly, so triathletes should be ary of pulling toestraps too tight (wiggling e toes and arching the foot inside the oe will alleviate discomfort). Standing up the pedals will help to relax the legs, opping the heel down as you do this to retch the calf and leaning forward in the right position to take pressure away from e lower back. Standing up is often done hen climbing hills; it gives an alternative ding position and breaks tedium. The ands are usually moved away from the ops and placed on the brake tops or en on the tops of the bars close to the em, and the arm strength can be more rectly used to climb the hills.

Using the Gears

The speed of pedalling that you are able to maintain depends on your fitness and leg strength, and also which gears you choose to use. Your choice of gears for any particular section of the race or training session will also depend on the terrain of the course and the weather conditions, particularly the wind speed.

The gear that you decide to ride in will govern how far you travel in one turn of the pedals. The gear ratio is 'the distance in inches travelled by the driving wheel for one revolution of the pedals' and is calculated as follows: wheel diameter in inches multiplied by the number of chainwheel teeth, divided by the number of teeth on the rear sprocket. This figure is then multiplied by π (3·1416) to adjust wheel diameter to wheel circumference. The bigger the

55   *The rear gear mechanism and sprocket.*

chainwheel, the bigger the gear; the bigger the sprocket, the smaller the gear. Almost all racing bikes now have a range of twelve gears as standard (two chainrings, six sprocket rings), some have fourteen (two chainrings, seven sprockets). However it is rare that all these gears would be available to the rider as some would be duplicated by the ratio of another chainring and sprocket, while some would pull the chain too far out of line – the bigger chainring and the biggest sprocket are an obvious example.

Some triathletes will attempt small hills without changing into a different gear, being prepared to lift themselves out of the saddle and push that much harder, while others will want to maintain a fast pedalling speed at all costs. On longer or steeper hills, all triathletes will have to make some adjustment to escape the build-up of lactic acid which will otherwise ensue due to a heavier anaerobic workload. The trade-off between speed and effort will have to be judged by each individual; many kilometres covered during training will give both the experience and confidence to make the correct decision during a race, and to be able to anticipate the reaction of your body and the sort of recovery that it will demand after a hill-climbing effort. A rapid and drastic change in respiration will indicate that the wrong gear has been chosen for that particular effort.

The same type of decision on gearing will have to be made when facing a windy course, whether to push a big gear into a headwind or to drop down and maintain a fast pedalling speed. The effects of a good aerodynamic position will be felt more in a strong wind. When you are in the happy position of having a strong wind behind you, it is possible to get into a high gear and still maintain a high pedalling rate.

Braking

For some cyclists, it is a point of honour n to use the brakes – this is not advisabl Brakes should be treated gently by an cipating problems and course difficultie which will require you to use them. A sha application of the brakes can separate yc from your machine! Try to apply the fro brake first, particularly on turns and benc (especially if they are downhill).

Breaking

Things can go wrong with machinery training and in racing. When it occurs training, it is a nuisance. When it occu during a race, it inevitably means that yc drop down the finishing order. It is impc tant to be able to fix at least minor repairs. triathlete would not wish to carry a fu repair kit during a race as it would not k practical. However, a triathlete should try avoid taking any chances with possib faulty equipment or mechanical problem by carrying out regular checks on equip ment, especially in the days before a rac always allowing sufficient time to repair replace any faults discovered. All movir parts should be greased and dirt-free. Th steering and transmission are particular prone to failure if not looked after properly

1. Take special care with the front ar rear gear mechanisms, bottom bracke chainring and rear sprockets, headset, ar pedals.
2. Check that the wheels are running tru and free, and that all spokes are adequate tightened.
3. Tyres should be looked at closely f any signs of cracking, splitting or bulging.
4. Look regularly at the brakes, handl bars and stem and all clips and straps.

Ensure that the gear levers are tight but ee-moving and responsive.

Don't forget your pump, your on-bike pair kit, and make sure your water bottle filled.

Finally, check tyre pressure.

Punctures can be mended or tubs hanged, and triathletes should be able to o this swiftly and efficiently. It is possible change a tubular tyre and re-inflate in nder three minutes which is not a great eal of time over a race period of perhaps vo or three hours. The choice of tubulars high pressures should also be decided ell before the event.

EXTRAS AND INNOVATIONS

As cycling is the most expensive drain on a triathlete's pocket, it is hardly surprising that it is also very technically innovative. This can be a boon to those seeking the exotic and esoteric but can also be expensive.

Helmets are compulsory for all events organised under the auspices of the BTA and for commonsense safety reasons they should also be worn during training. It is likely that in the near future regulations governing the type of helmet worn will come into force, with special reference to cushioning and the ability of the helmet to withstand stress on impact. Aerodynamic

g 56   The clothing and sundries for the cycle section.

Figs 57–59   Hi-tech hits the sport. Note the disc wheel and aerodynamic helmets in both pictures.

Fig 60   Bikes are the most expensive part of a triathlete's equipment.
Transition areas contain, literally, hundreds of thousands of pounds
worth of machinery.

mets in the so-called 'teardrop' shape
: available at the moment and are very
pular and effective in shaving off those
:ra seconds. Triathletes should check the
'ety aspects of any helmet selected
fore making a final purchase.

Disc wheels are another very easy
:thod of relieving you of your money.
Iain, they are effective but the expense
Ist be balanced against the time saved.
perienced triathletes estimate up to a
nute saved over the standard 40km
urse. In strong cross winds, however,
:y are more a liability than an advantage.
A triathlete has to compete in all weather
nditions, and also has to be prepared to
in in all weather conditions. However,
:re are times when it is dangerous as well
highly unpleasant to train outside on the
ke. Rollers have long been available for
Joor training, and although there is little
Iing resistance, they have been used for
lance, cadence and stamina training.
Over the last few years, wind trainers
ve become available. With these, the
nt wheel is removed and the bike fixed
the front forks and the bottom bracket to
sturdy metal frame. The rear wheel is
aced on a circular metal roller and is
ady for action. When used for training,
: ride more closely simulates that of the
ad, with more effort required as a higher
r bigger) gear is selected. For keeping
curate time splits for interval type train-
J, or for use when recovering from injury,
:se are highly beneficial.

Computers which are mounted on the
Indlebars and give a quick, easy read-out
speed and distance covered and other
:tails, have become *de rigueur* in the last
w seasons. They can be invaluable for
Iining, although caution should be exer-
sed as to their usefulness in races when
:y can become a dominating factor, and

Fig 61   The bicycle is mounted on a wind-
          trainer.

stop the triathlete from thinking for himself
and taking into account other extraneous
features.

The latest addition to the space-age
technology of cycling is the new design
handlebars, with the 'Scott' and the 'Aero
One' the most popular. Most of the world's
top triathletes use one type or the other. The
basic idea of the bars is to more closely
simulate the aerodynamic position achieved
in downhill skiing, and they were first
thought of by an American ski-coach with a
great interest in cycling. The arms are held
close to the body and the head is near to
the hands. The position is certainly less
stable but does give the benefit of stretching
out the lower back more than a conventional

Cycling

Fig 62   Gavin Attwood on Aero 1
          handlebars.

Fig 63   Holland's Irma Zwartkruis uses the
          Scott bars.

riding position. If these bars are used, it is important to attain the correct position – as Ironman champion, New Zealander Erin Baker says, 'There are a lot of people using them to look good who don't really know how to ride them'.

Triathletes will want to try out and experiment with these kinds of equipment but whatever is chosen or discarded there is no short cut to racing success, and no substitute for fitness attained by spending time on the bike.

4 Running

'There are a lot of great runners humbled when they get off the bike.'

Dave Scott
Six-times Hawaii Ironman winner.

Many aspiring triathletes come into the sport with a running background, indeed most everybody has run at some time in their lives. Of the three disciplines, it is the least complicated. *But* – and it is a big but – the sensation of putting one foot in front of the other after first having swum and then having cycled for an hour or more is an athletic activity which may only remotely resemble the smooth flowing action experienced when running as a single sport. The circular motion of cycling and the blood pooling in the cycling muscles is not the best warm-up for a 10km run and the fatigue that triathletes bring with them into a run may often be severe.

However the ability to overcome that fatigue and to run fast and efficiently can be a major factor in successfully completing an event in a time acceptable to the athlete.

The runner who has neglected his or her swimming and cycling training will be at a major disadvantage, even when entering their specialist discipline. Extra energy will have already been used to compensate for a weak upper body in swimming and poorly developed quadriceps in cycling. So even with the uncomplicated activity of running, we can see that in triathlon it is essential to look at the whole event as well as the component parts.

There are no short cuts to becoming a good triathlon runner in triathlon events; technique, speed, strength, and mobility training together with an awareness of the specific requirements of triathlon running will all lead to longer and faster performances.

SPEED

When triathletes with similar levels of aerobic and anaerobic endurance compete against each other going into the final discipline, it is usually their basic running speed which decides the outcome. Speed is an essential attribute for any endurance event and it is as important to develop this aspect of fitness as it is to develop stamina.

Running speed is related to how fast the legs move and how much distance is covered with each stride, summed up as:

Speed = Stride length × Stride rate

Obviously, an increase in the length of the stride will lead to increased speed, provided that the rate of striding does not slow. Success in improving this will be largely governed by range of movement in the joints and strength in the running muscle groups.

TECHNIQUE AND THE RUNNING ACTION

The technique of endurance running is a modification of sprinting, but as relaxation

Running

Fig 64 *Mark Marabini shows that excellent running form can be maintained during a triathlon event.*

the thigh begins to move downwards. The whole leg then sweeps backwards and downwards until the foot strikes the ground again.

The upper body remains upright or leaning slightly forward. The arm action is often forgotten but should match the leg action with the left arm coming forward at the same time as the right leg and vice versa in an equal and opposite action and reaction; even though the shoulders may be tight and sore after the swimming and cycling disciplines. The arm movement should be kept relaxed and rhythmic, moving backwards and forwards in a straight line with the hands loosely cupped and the thumbs resting on the fingers. Since you will almost certainly feel tight and stiff at some point during the run, it may be advisable to roll the neck and the head around from time to time, and to shake out the arms to overcome this.

and saving energy are so important in triathlon, the action of running has to be more compact to eliminate unnecessary expenditure of energy.

As with the arms in swimming, there is a propulsive phase and a recovery phase with the legs in running. The propulsive phase starts as soon as the foot makes contact with the ground during a running stride. The whole of the body weight is carried by the foot as the hips and trunk pass over the foot, and the hip, knee and ankle stretch out to push the runner forward.

The recovery phase begins with the foot breaking contact with the ground. The foot is pulled upwards to the backside and the thigh swings forward and through until it is parallel, or nearly so, to the ground. The lower part of the leg then comes forward as

SKILLS AND DRILLS

Running at a good speed is a complex movement which has to be learned to be done efficiently. Running is a skill, albeit one which is practised daily by millions of people, and like any skill it can be improved by attention to detail. As it is a complex movement, it cannot be learned in one piece, that is just by running fast as all that would be done would be to ingrain existing faults. Hence the use of drills which are designed to develop the running action and are commonly used by sprinters. Triathletes are not sprinters, but if the aim of the game is to run fast in races, then every possible advantage which can be gained must be explored. Good execution of drill requires co-ordination and balance and may have to be learned initially by working

Fig 65   Great Britain International Cathy Bow exits the transition area with
no loss of speed. Behind her a male triathlete is suffering the
effects of bloodpooling.

through each one separately in slow motion. Drills isolate and concentrate on only one aspect of running at a time and are carried out for very short distances, usually between 40 and 100m. Some fundamental learning principles have to be observed and the triathlete should ensure that he or she is not tired, stiff or injured when embarking upon new drills. The most important components of the running action are: high lift of the thigh; paw down and back of the lead leg; full extension of the rear leg; full and straight range of arm movement; high kickback. Many track runners at all distances will incorporate these drills into their warm-up to try to establish the above components.

1. *Long rear leg.* A singular effort is made to push the ground away and to leave the foot in contact with the ground a fraction longer than usual.

2. *High knee action.* The knees are pulled higher than usual while still trying to maintain an erect body position.

3. *Leg reach out.* As the lower leg reaches forward, it is pushed slightly further and then the foot is consciously pulled back to strike the ground.

4. *Bounding.* The entire running action is exaggerated and slowed down with the athlete lifting high between steps and floating foot plants.

5. *High arms.* The forward lift of the arms is exaggerated, the opposite leg will follow and lift higher.

6. *Rear arms.* As the runner moves down the track, the elbows are pulled backward and upwards without the shoulders lifting.

7. *Close arms.* The elbows are kept close to the sides of the body while running, with the arms swinging backwards and forwards.

Variations in Training

Often, people who are not interested in or associated with sport try to ridicule the training efforts of sportspeople by asking 'Why do you do it?', 'What do you get out of it?', or the usual, 'Don't you get bored?' Running comes in for more than its fair share of criticism regarding boredom. But is the athlete who makes the training boring, not the activity itself. Certainly, if the running training is the same every day, over the same distance, over the same course, at the same time, then it will become boring. With running, compared with swimming where the training has to be confined largely to the pool, and even with cycling where the rider has to stay on the roads, the runner has the freedom to go anywhere to train with a choice of the roads, the country or the track. Running on the road or in the country doesn't have to be at a single speed slow plod; try varying the speed with accelerations at every fifth or tenth lamppost, going out with a training partner and letting them choose the route and pace – even turning up at your local running track and training with different partners can make a big difference to the enjoyment of training.

Doing some 'fartlek' (Swedish for speed play) training can be particularly exhilarating and extremely beneficial in combatting the varying demands experienced during a race. Make it a structured fartlek by deciding before you start that you will attack every hill hard, or that you will sprint after every corner, or that you will run fast for one lamppost and then two up to a maximum of ten. The speed and the challenge you have set yourself will ensure that there is no boredom, and certainly the training run will appear to go a lot faster than usual. It is all too easy in a race to accept the accumulated

Hip Rotation

From a standing position, with hands on hips, push hips forward, to the side, to the back and to the left, to create a circular movement (clockwise). Repeat exercise in anti-clockwise order.

Quadriceps Stretch

Standing on your right leg, reach back and grasp left ankle with left hand and pull ankle back (not to the side) until you feel the stretch in the front of the thigh. Repeat with right leg.

Hamstring Stretch (Standing)

Stand with feet together and hands at your side. Drop head forward and, keeping knees straight, roll down the spine, one vertebra at a time. Reach down to touch toes, hold for 4 counts, then repeat.

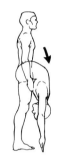

Groin Stretch

Place hands on hips. Lunge forward with right foot, turning left foot at right angle. Then shift weight forward over right knee, keeping body upright so that you feel a stretch on the inside of your left thigh. Repeat with left foot forward.

Side stretch

In a standing position, with feet 30cm (12in) apart, place left hand on left hip. Stretch right hand above head and pull over head to the left-hand side to feel stretch down right-hand side. Hold for 4 counts, then repeat on other side.

Upper Trunk Rotation

With legs astride, place hands on hips, bend forward moving trunk to the left-hand side, to the back and to the right-hand side in a circular movement. Repeat in opposite direction.

Hamstring, Calf and Achilles Tendon Stretch

Put straight arms against a wall and lean your body on them at a 30° angle. Put right leg forward, keeping left heel on ground – feel hamstring and calf being stretched. Then bend left knee and stretch the achilles tendon. Repeat with other leg.

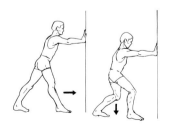

Fig 66   Mobility exercises.

Running

tiredness built up during the swimming and cycling phases and to fall into a slow plod without making any real effort to break out of the rut. Playing around with speed during a training run will get you used to upping your speed when you are tired and don't want to. Many triathlons are won and lost on the running phases; they are lost not by a lack of stamina but rather by an inability to accept the challenge of another athlete running past you. It is crucial that you are prepared to accept that challenge by having experienced the sensation of increasing speed when tired during training sessions.

Mobility

Strength and mobility play an important part in the length and speed of the stride when running. However, with a triathlete's busy training schedule, there are aspects – usually mobility – which can be easily neglected in preference to 'getting the miles in'. This will be to the detriment of the triathlete and may lead to shortened stride length, incorrect running action and even a greater likelihood of injury. Triathletes do have an advantage over pure runners as their more complex schedules in three separate sports will give greater mobility, but it should be remembered that mobility naturally decreases from the late teens unless remedial action is taken to forestall it. Mobility work should be undergone at every training session during the warm-up if the triathlete is to maximise his or her potential.

From the section on 'Technique and the Running Action' above, it is easily seen that the degree to which a triathlete can develop his running action will depend to some extent on his mobility and ability to perform joint actions through a wide range of movement. Without this mobility in the joints used in running, a shortened stride length and a poor technique become likely. A good running technique involves the flexion and extension of the ankle, knee, hip and elbow joints, and some rotation in the joints. Poor mobility inhibits this flexion and extension and can also increase the likelihood of injury by damaging muscles, tendons, ligaments and other connective tissue by the athlete attempting to exceed the normal range of movement. Stress can also accumulate by placing extra work on muscles to accommodate an athlete's lack of mobility. Good mobility is particularly important for triathlon as it encourages efficient movement in the last discipline of a race when cumulative fatigue is being felt by the tired competitor. A good level of mobility will reduce energy demands.

Mobility work can be divided into active and passive exercises. During an active exercise the athlete stretches his own muscles, while during a passive exercise the athlete relaxes and allows a partner to stretch his muscles for him. The swinging and bouncing type of warm-up exercises often seen are not to be encouraged as they can actually cause injury rather than prevent it if they are carried out before active or passive stretching. If passive stretching is chosen, the athlete should take care to have an experienced partner who is aware of the dangers of forcing a muscle to stretch too far and cause injury. When performing stretching exercises, the athlete should slowly stretch out as far as possible and then hold that position for a count of ten seconds before slowly relaxing and then repeating. Experienced athletes in many sports are able to concentrate on relaxing the muscle even while stretching it. Mobility exercises will feel more comfortable if performed after an easy jog which will raise the temperature of the body.

SHOES

Equally important in the avoidance of injury is the choice of a good pair of shoes.

Brightly coloured shorts, vest, tracksuit and trisuit may look good and make you feel good but a good pair of shoes will help to make you run 'good'. Most specialist running shops are happy to give advice, and it is safer in the initial stages to buy from a local shop with help from someone experienced in runners' needs, than it is to send away for a pair of mail order shoes which may be slightly cheaper than buying retail, but could cause problems later on. A training shoe is a better buy than a racing flat to start with, as the extra cushioning in the shoe will reduce the risk of injury particularly if you are on the heavy side. Go

for a shoe that feels comfortable and gives you good support both underneath and on the sides. The running boom has led to a corresponding boom in the manufacture of running shoes and you can now buy them for every conceivable weight, distance, type of foot plant and training conditions. If you are tempted by the ultra-light racing shoes, just remember that the 5-minute miles that you might be able to push out during your local league 3 mile road races might be a little ambitious at the end of a 3 hour triathlon. When you do find a pair of shoes which are comfortable to train in, it is tempting to hang on to them as long as possible. Unfortunately, shoes wear out and to continue to wear them after they have served their purpose is to invite injury caused by a wrong foot plant aggravated

Fig 67   The clothing for running.

by wear and tear on the soles of the shoes. There are several 'shoe glues' and 'shoe goos' which will repair the soles to a certain extent, but however effective they are, they will not be able to adequately replace the cushioning and support supplied in a newer shoe. Savings made on running shoes are false savings.

Other items of running clothing are detailed in Chapter 8.

5 Back-to-Back and Crosstraining

The two terms 'crosstraining', and 'back-to-back training', have in the past been frequently and incorrectly used as synonymous with each other. One possible explanation is that when triathlon was greeted by the aficionados upon its arrival from America, new terms were welcomed as an extension of the exotic and esoteric sport, without the devotees bothering to really find out what the terms meant! However, both concepts are closely linked and are important parts of the sport, and so deserve clarification.

CROSSTRAINING

The classic definition of crosstraining is that when one muscle group is exercised, a corresponding muscle group also shows increased strength even if it is kept stationary, so long as the motor nerves to the inactive part are uninjured. A footballer with a broken leg in a plaster cast will not lose all his strength in this leg, for example, if the other uninjured leg is made to maintain exercising. Even as long as fifty years ago physiologists were discovering that training one muscle group resulted in significant improvements in the (symmetrical) partner group on the corresponding other side of the body, even if unexercised. The term they gave to this was 'cross education', which applied both to skill training and strength improvement. The training required in the active limb needed to be done at an intense level to provide the equivalent effect of an easy training session on the matching unexercised limb. Although it is still partly unclear why this occurs, it is thought that the nerves which cross over from the muscles in the active limb to the inactive muscle on the other side of the body are stimulated sufficiently during overload (high intensity) training to create an effect. The body's system is very much interdependent, being a complex interconnected mechanism rather than a series of independent parts.

In triathlon terms, this has come to be summarised as the benefits and improvements to one sport which carry over from training in another. In the early days of triathlon great claims were made that might make one think that all you had to do was to swim hard and your cycling and running would improve! We know a little more than that now. There are great benefits from training in more than one discipline which can be categorised as follows:

1. Building and maintaining a good, strong aerobic capacity.
2. Increased flexibility from training and using other muscles than would be required in a single sport.
3. An avoidance of injury from the 'overuse' syndrome. Certainly every distance runner has had to take time away from training because of sore muscles or locked knees.
4. No boredom!

5. A maintenance of strong antagonistic muscles.

Although it may seem obvious, all the above points are related and interlinked, as with triathlon itself.

Aerobic Effect

Because triathlons are essentially aerobic – even the so-called 'sprint' distance of 1500m swim; 40km cycle; and 10km run will take the experts almost two hours, and novices as much or more than double that time – any training that is undergone aerobically is going to apply to all three disciplines. The respiratory system will be the first to benefit from the crossover effects, but there will also be a carry over to the circulatory system and, to a limited extent, in the area of muscle use.

Any aerobic training, be it swimming, cycling, running or whatever, will increase the amount of oxygen getting from the lungs to the muscles in action via the bloodstream. However, only the muscles being exercised at any particular time will be affected, therefore muscular transfer between disciplines is very restricted, and only muscles which are used in more than one activity will receive any benefit. There is some transfer of muscle use; hill running and cycling on the flat, and hill cycle climbing and flat running do use some of the same muscles so there will be a crossover effect here.

What we do know is that working out aerobically carries over the type of training effect between the same type of muscle fibres, distance training works the slow twitch fibres and the efficiency of these will improve whatever the aerobic training method used.

Flexibility

Distance runners particularly and professional cyclists to a large extent are notorious for their lack of mobility and lack of flexibility. Even international swimmers with tremendous upper body suppleness may be lacking in leg mobility. The reason may be obvious; that these sportsmen and women choose to exercise only the muscle groups needed by their sport. The triathlete, even if he or she does not always stretch and warm-up as he should, will still expect to get the benefits of extra flexibility by exercising muscle groups which a single sport exponent would not use. However it is not easy to gain flexibility, especially when coming from a single sport background of cycling or running where patterns of movement may have already been established. Other factors may also affect the amount of mobility in an individual including genetic make-up, muscular development, the amount of muscle fibre elasticity that you have, previous sporting background which may add or detract from the flexibility gained, age, and of course, how hard you work at it. A word of caution here though; if gaining flexibility becomes so important that you are in stress or pain trying to get it, you could be working against yourself and will break down with muscle aches or even injury; as with any training, a gradual increase in the work-load is the way to go.

Injury

The high quality athlete in most sports walks the thin line between superfitness and breaking down when starting to increase the amount of training in time or in intensity. Certainly in running, the stress put on joints and the continual pressure on the muscles and joints from the downward

rce being exerted with every foot plant
akes walking the tightrope of superfitness
delicate operation.

Paradoxically, the superfit athlete is often
n the point of breaking down from injury.

The benefits of crosstraining where one
iscipline does not dominate can allay this.
ncreased aerobic capacity comes about
om any of the three component activities,
nd each set of muscles does not have to
e overused. Great care must still be taken
vhen adding speed training to the sche-
lule though as an increase here can
uickly become an injury without adequate
reparation or warming up.

If a triathlete becomes injured and is
nable to take part or train in one discipline,
erobic fitness can still be maintained by
vorking out in the other two disciplines.
his has already transferred itself to other
ports so that when a runner is injured, they
ake a leaf out of the triathlete's book and
jo for a swim or a cycle. Injured runners in
america have made use of swimming pools
nd the cushioning effects of water for
nore than thirty years. Apart from actually
wimming, runners have worn buoyant
ests and have been able to go through the
notions of running in the water without their
eet ever having to touch any hard surface,
nd thereby avoiding any pounding.

Boredom

One thing that you certainly don't suffer
vith in the sport of triathlon is boredom.
Professional cyclists can spend the greater
part of every day in the saddle, thousands
upon thousands of serious distance runners
cover more than 150 kilometres (100 miles)
each week, competitive swimmers can be
n the pool twice a day covering five
housand metres each time. The triathlete
has the best of all three worlds: a different

environment; different training companions;
a solitary workout if wanted, can all be
accommodated in a comprehensive training
schedule. If one discipline does become
intolerable, the alternative is always there.
A day's missed training in one sport can
always be caught up, so long as other
training continues.

Antagonistic Muscles

Movements in your body are governed by
the *agonist* muscles which initiate this movement by shortening. The *antagonist* muscles
are those that lengthen and oppose the
movement. One of the main reasons for
injuries occuring in single sports is that the
antagonist muscles are not strong enough to
work efficiently against the agonists. In triathlon training, it is more likely that the opposing
muscles are strong by having been worked
in a different discipline.

When you are running, your hamstrings
at the back of the upper legs are the main
agonists and thus shorten while the quadriceps at the top front of the thighs are the
antagonists and lengthen. When you cycle,
the opposite happens; the quadriceps
become the prime movers and shorten
while the hamstrings, acting in opposition,
lengthen. The same action and reaction is
occurring below the knees, albeit on the
opposite sides from the upper leg muscles.
In running, the calf muscles on the rear of
the legs are shortening and the shin muscles are lengthening. In cycling, the shin
muscles are shortening and the calf muscles stretching out.

SPORTS SPECIFICITY

It must not be thought that crosstraining
is the panacea to all sports improvement.

It patently isn't. Performers in a single sport need to spend all their available time concentrating on their speciality. Sports specificity requires that to be a better swimmer or cyclist or runner, then swimming or cycling or running training alone will better develop and improve that individual sport. Ability in one sport does not automatically programme an athlete for top class performance in another. With only a limited amount of time available in any one day, training for a different sport will only take away from developing those skills and strengths required for one's own sport.

What can be done by those athletes who do have unlimited time at their disposal is to add to their training by taking part in other activities, sometimes going directly on to working out in a different sport after training on your own. There is a limit to the amount of running training, for example, that can be done before the body rebels and begins to break down. There is no doubt that running is the most physically taxing of triathlon's three disciplines. However, the endurance factor can be brought into play here by continuing to work out aerobically on cycling or swimming. This continuous training in one sport followed by another is what is known as back-to-back training.

BACK-TO-BACK TRAINING

A triathlete's first aim is to build an endurance base. In the very early days there can often be a sense of frustration when the athlete wants to keep training but commonsense, sore muscles and an awareness of capabilities tells him or her to back off. To repeat the golden rule; make haste slowly. However there is a case to be made for continuing training in another activity, if it is specific muscle soreness that is to be avoided rather than a sense of sheer fatigue. If the athlete is very tired then little is to be gained from continuing to train; rest is at least as important in this instance.

We know that one of the fascinations of triathlon both for the competitor and the spectator is seeing how the participants cope with the demands of the three different disciplines. When an athlete is experienced and has raced many times, it becomes less important to train back-to-back as the frequency of racing causes the body to adapt, but in the early days when the transitions are quite literally a shock to the system, it makes good sense both mentally and physically to follow training in one discipline directly by another. The intensity of these back-to-back sessions should be monitored carefully in order to avoid injury and mental staleness.

The normal order of a triathlon is the swim, followed by the cycle, followed by the run. Some back-to-back training sessions will need to be done in this order swim/bike, or bike/run, to acclimatise the body to the race's demands. However, this is not always essential and many productive sessions can be undertaken by run bike, swim/run or indeed any combination of two or three activities. In many cases it makes good sense in terms of time management – and time is always at a premium for triathletes – for sessions to follow on directly from each other. If you live within running distance of your local swimming pool, why not jog down there carrying your swimming costume and towel in a back pack? Certainly it will feel uncomfortable for a short time when you pull on damp running clothes for the return journey, but you will have saved a lot of time and you will have exercised aerobically for longer than by splitting the training sessions up. If the pool is too far for running, then jump on your bike; the same extra aerobic effect is gained and for the cycle home there is some knowledge of what can be expected during a race. It is worth having a look at the different back-to-back sessions and their effects individually.

SWIM/CYCLE

This session prepares you for the effects of blood pooling in the arms and for the sensations that you would expect during a race as you exit the swim/cycle transition area. As most of the muscular output of swimming is in the arms and upper body, this is where the blood is directed during exercise. When the triathlete gets on to the cycle section the blood has to be rapidly redirected to the legs.

SWIM/RUN

This session will give similar benefits to that of the swim/cycle. The arm blood pooling will have to redirect to the legs.

CYCLE/RUN

This is considered the hardest transition. The legs are already fatigued from being worked hard during the cycle stage, and then they are immediately called upon to work even harder for the run section. The blood is already centred in the legs, but mainly in the quadriceps on the front of the thighs. As you race out of transition and into the run, it is a truly remarkable sensation for the first timer. Nothing that you have heard or have been told adequately prepares you for the awful feeling of having lost control of your legs. The blood is urgently required in

Fig 68   Sarah Springman is used to the feeling of cycle/run transitions.

running's prime movers, the hamstrings, and the first few minutes while the blood transfers is not a pleasant sensation. However it does get better and easier with experience and practice does help greatly to ease the discomfort. The ability to run well during a triathlon race is not always directly related to how well the individual can run, in a single event, as far more depends on the individual's ability to cope with the accumulated fatigue and the management of the ensuing discomfort and pain.

RUN/SWIM

Transfer of blood pooling will be experienced here as the leg centralisation will have to redirect to the upper body. Many athletes who have run to the pool in order to save valuable training time have commented on how they need a longer warm-up than usual for their arms to acknowledge that they belong to them and to perform as required.

CYCLE/SWIM

This can produce a similar situation to the run/swim workout although the effects are not normally as marked.

RUN/CYCLE

This session can be particularly effective for three reasons.

The risk of injury undertaken by any long distance runner attempting a big mileage can be lessened by shortening the run and immediately transferring to the bike. Particularly when the run needs to be for a longer period than two hours, when preparing for a marathon for example, the chances of an overuse injury are dramatically increased. Many athletes have experimented with dropping the run time down to ninety minutes and then getting straight on to a wind trainer mounted cycle for three quarters of an hour. This also has the added benefit of increasing the total training time.

The aerobic effect of training will be maintained by the immediate transfer to the bike.

The usual stiffness that follows a longer than usual training run will be dispersed to a considerable extent by allowing the waste by-products of exercise that are accumulated in the legs by running to be washed away with the less traumatic action of cycling.

It should be remembered that even if the immediate effects of back-to-back training are not felt, it is an extremely taxing and fatiguing method of training, and athletes particularly in the early stages of experimenting with it, should be prepared for feeling very fatigued, if not immediately then at some time later in the day. Rest can make all the difference.

6 Exercise Physiology for Triathletes

Triathlon is an endurance activity. Even so-called 'sprint events' last for an hour or more. The three disciplines of swimming, cycling and running require the muscles to alternately contract and relax, and although it is not the purpose of this book to enter into a discourse of the body's anatomy and physiology, it is relevant to discuss the aspects of exercise physiology which relate to endurance activities.

Every time a muscle is brought into use, the muscle fibres contract, shortening the muscle length; and every time the muscle fibres are brought into play, they use energy in the form of a substance called adenosine triphosphate (ATP). Without ATP the muscles cannot move, therefore a constant supply of ATP is required.

This ATP is a molecule consisting of an adenosine atom surrounded by three phosphate atoms. When the muscle fibres shorten along their lengths, ATP is used and as a result it loses one of its phosphate atoms and changes into another substance called adenosine diphosphate (ADP).

When this occurs the muscle fibres can no longer shorten and movement cannot take place. To be able to swim, cycle or run, then, the muscles need a constant supply of ATP. The aim of all endurance training be it triathlon, swimming, running, cycling or cross-country skiing is to ensure that the muscles have a sufficient supply of energy in the form of ATP. The energy can be provided either aerobically (sufficient oxygen can be supplied by the lungs) or anaerobically (for which there is an insufficient oxygen supply). Although triathlon competing and training may be largely aerobic, particularly for the beginner, there are instances when the anaerobic systems – both lactic and alactic – may be called upon.

THE AEROBIC SYSTEM

So long as there is an adequate supply of oxygen to the muscles, carbohydrates in the form of glycogen and fats in the form of free fatty acids can be metabolised to make ATP. Helped by oxidative enzymes to release the energy, the glycogen and fats reduce to carbon dioxide and water, producing in the process a number of ATP molecules.

The carbohydrate which is stored in the muscles in the form of glycogen is converted into pyruvic acid by a process known as glycolysis which produces three ATP molecules. The pyruvic acid combines

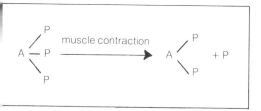

Fig 69 The chemical reaction which occurs as muscle fibres shorten.

with the oxygen in the muscles (within cells known as mitochondria, the 'engine room' of the muscles) to produce carbon dioxide and water. This produces a further thirty-six ATP molecules, making thirty-nine in all produced from one unit of carbohydrate by aerobic metabolism.

Fats are also stored to be available in the muscles as free fatty acids, and can also be taken up by the mitochondria to combine with the oxygen to produce thirty-six ATP molecules. The oxidation of fats produces thirty-six ATP molecules compared with the thirty-nine produced when the fuel is carbohydrate which explains why twelve per cent extra oxygen is used to produce the same amount of energy from fats as from carbohydrates. Fats in the body are in almost inexhaustible supply when compared to carbohydrate, and although they are not as rich an energy source it must be remembered that the available carbohydrate can usually supply only enough energy to meet demand for up to two hours of endurance activity such as swimming, cycling or running.

THE ANAEROBIC SYSTEM

Lactic

When there is not enough oxygen in the muscle to meet all the energy demands through the aerobic system, energy can be made available through the anaerobic metabolism of carbohydrate. As in the aerobic system, the muscle glycogen is converted to pyruvic acid through glycolysis. However, as there is no oxygen available to combine with the pyruvic acid, the mitochondria cells do not take up the pyruvic acid. The pyruvic acid converts to lactic acid, a waste product of anaerobic exercise, which unlike the waste products of aerobic exercise are not easily dispersed. Lactic acid has to wait until oxygen becomes available before it can be reconverted to pyruvate or glycogen. While there is this time-lag, the lactic acid accumulated in the muscle can spill over into the bloodstream and its presence has a negative influence on performance.

The lactic acid remaining in the muscle inhibits the enzymes which enable glycogen to be converted to energy anaerobically and also inhibits the muscle from contracting. If there is too much lactate present in the muscle, the triathlete will be forced to slow down or even to stop altogether if the level becomes too high. Obviously, an overproduction of lactic acid is a limiting factor on performance. However if instant speed is required, for example at the end of an event to outsprint a rival, the large amount of energy needed can be made available quickly. Anaerobic energy production is far quicker than aerobic energy production.

Alactic

There is a tiny amount of ATP stored in our muscles which would last a mere four seconds if the athlete exercised to maximum stress. If the exercise lasts over four seconds, then fresh ATP is needed from one of the energy systems. There is a substance called creatine phosphate (CP) within the muscles' other phosphates and this contains an immediate source of available ATP. The ADP created when an ATP loses one of its phosphates combines with the CP to reconvert itself to ATP. It does so by borrowing one of the CP's phosphates as shown in Fig 70.

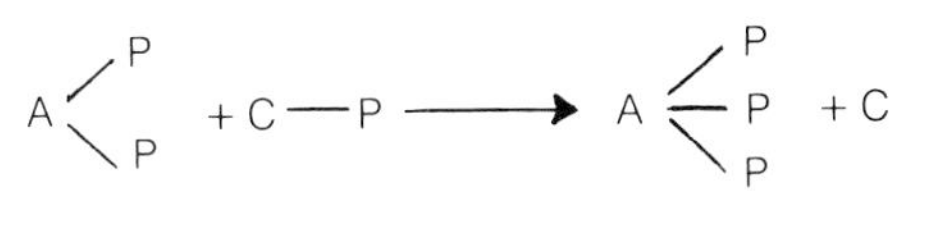

$$A \big\langle{}^{P}_{P} + C - P \longrightarrow A \big\langle{}^{P}_{P}{}_{P} + C$$

Fig 70   Reconversion from ADP to ATP.

This method of producing ATP is short-ved as the muscle's store of CP is limited. t is only about three times the size of the ATP store and therefore lasts for about welve seconds.

To produce more ATP the muscles have o break down either the carbohydrate or at available in the body. As we have seen n the aerobic system and the lactic anaerobic system, carbohydrates can be broken down in both the aerobic and anaerobic metabolisms, but fat can only be broken down in the aerobic process.

Although the alactic anaerobic energy system can provide energy quickly, the store of that energy is exhausted almost immediately and in an endurance sport such as triathlon the use of the alactic anaerobic system is very limited. It should be noted however, that the three energy systems do not work independently of each other, with one starting as the other finishes, but all three systems contribute some ATP o meet the demands of the activity from the start. It is the duration and intensity of swimming, cycling or running which deter-mine the relative importance of the three systems.

THE OXYGEN TRANSPORT SYSTEM

For any race, whether individual sport or triathlon, the longer it continues, the more important the aerobic system becomes for providing the energy required. In races lasting for around fifteen minutes, about eighty percent of the energy requirements are supplied by the aerobic system; for around thirty minutes, this grows to about ninety per cent. When one looks at the time taken for the majority of triathlon events, the realisation that the aerobic system is of paramount importance becomes evident.

If energy is to be provided by the aerobic system, a constant supply of oxygen has to be made available to the mitochondria cells within the muscles. The oxygen is con-tained in the air that is breathed into the lungs through the windpipe. The lungs are divided into two sac-like parts. Each branch of the windpipe keeps subdividing until they eventually end in the tiny thin walled sacs known as the alveoli. These are surrounded by a mass of extremely fine blood vessels called capillaries. It is in the alveoli that the oxygen transfers from the air and through the thin walls into the blood-stream. As the oxygen passes into the blood, carbon dioxide is passed out of the bloodstream and into the lungs for expira-tion. The rate of breathing is low at rest but increases with exercise to help take in more oxygen.

The blood which passes through the capillaries surrounding the alveoli is forced around the pulmonary (lung) circulatory system by the pumping action of the heart. The heart is divided into two halves, each of which is split into an upper and lower chamber; the upper is the atrium and the lower is the ventricle. The two sides are separated by a thick muscular wall. Between the atrium and the ventricle is a valve which regulates the flow of blood in one direction only when the heart muscles contract.

Blood from the body's general or systemic circulatory system enters the right atrium depleted of oxygen. The blood in the right atrium is pushed down into the right ventricle and is then forced round the pulmonary system as the heart contracts and squeezes blood out of the right ventricle. As the blood passes over the lungs, carbon dioxide is off-loaded and fresh supplies of oxygen are taken on. The blood then re-enters the heart through the left atrium and goes down into the left ventricle before being pumped round the body's systemic circulatory system.

The greater the volume of blood that can be pumped round the systemic system, the more oxygen that is available to the mitochondria. The amount of blood pumped round the body by the heart in a minute is known as the cardiac output. The cardiac output is the volume of blood which is pumped out each time the heart contracts multiplied by the heart rate:

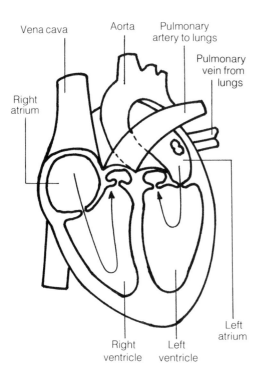

Fig 71   The heart.

Cardiac output = Stroke volume × Heart rate

The heart can be trained just like any other muscle, to make it stronger and to increase the volume of blood which it forces out with each beat. When this occurs, the rate at which the heart beats at rest and at any specific exercise rate falls. A greater volume of blood is now being circulated at a set heart rate which supplies more oxygen to the muscles. As the oxygen demands at rest and at a specific exercise rate stay the same, a lower heart rate will be able to supply the oxygen required.

The oxygen in the blood is carried by the haemoglobin which is contained within the red blood cells. The concentration of haemoglobin in men is usually 15·8g per 100ml of blood; in females the concentration is 13·7g per 100ml. The haemoglobin retains the oxygen until it reaches the muscles through another fine network of capillaries. These capillaries spread throughout the muscles making it possible for the myoglobin contained in the muscle cells to attract away from the haemoglobin in the bloodstream. The oxygen attracted from the bloodstream is used in the mitochondria to oxidise fuel. The carbon dioxide waste product of that chemical reaction is then deposited in the blood stream and carried via the heart to the lungs.

Maximal Oxygen Uptake

There is a limit to the amount of oxygen that can be carried to and used by the muscles. The amount of oxygen being used can be measured by using special equipment which compares the amount of oxygen being breathed in with the amount being breathed out. The difference between the wo gives the amount of oxygen used by the body. This is known as the oxygen uptake. The maximum amount of oxygen that the body can use is known as the maximal oxygen uptake, or 'VO_2 max'. An athlete's VO_2 max is taken as the amount of oxygen (measured in litres) used in one minute. To enable comparisons to be made between athletes, the value is divided by body weight to give a relative value expressed in millilitres of oxygen used per minute per kilogram of body-weight (ml/min/kg). This assessment is a commonly used way of indicating aerobic fitness and of predicting performances in endurance activities. VO_2 max scores can vary widely according to age, sex and fitness and averages are hard to give. However, young fairly fit men might hope to score over 40ml/kg/min with a woman scoring around 10ml less. Top class endurance athletes would hope to score in the upper 70s or even into the 80s, again with top class women athletes scoring 10ml less.

THRESHOLDS OF TRAINING

Aerobic Threshold

Physiologists estimate that aerobic capacity can be improved by up to thirty or forty per cent by training regularly, continuously, at the correct intensity and for sufficient time. However, life can be very unfair, and the single most important factor in having basic, good aerobic fitness is your genetic make-up. The body has to be put under stress if any adaptations to training are to occur. The workload has to push the athlete beyond his aerobic threshold if changes are to occur as a result of his endurance training. There will not be any effect if the training load is of such a low intensity that it does not reach the aerobic threshold.

The aerobic threshold is a percentage of the athlete's VO_2 max, which can be expressed as the heart rate which correlates with this. The heart rate increases in relation to the intensity of exercise, making it a good indicator of training stress. The Karvonen formula gives the following equation to indicate the correct aerobic training threshold:

Heart rate = 70% × (Maximum heart rate − Resting heart rate) + Resting heart rate (It is assumed that maximum heart rate is 220 − athlete's age, although this is by no means always true).

As an example, let us examine a mythical 30-year-old triathlete who has a resting heart rate of 60 beats per minute. One formula would then look like this:

$$
\begin{aligned}
\text{Heart rate} &= 70\% \times (220 - 30 - 60) + 60 \\
&= 70\% \times 130 + 60 \\
&= 91 + 60 \\
&= 151
\end{aligned}
$$

A quicker, but less accurate way of working out the aerobic threshold is to take 70% of your maximum heart rate, which, for our mythical triathlete would indicate a training level of 133 beats. This rough check does not take into account the resting heart rate which is, of course, a much better indicator of aerobic fitness.

As the triathlete becomes fitter and his resting pulse rate drops, say to 40 beats per minute, Karvonen's formula would indicate a training level of 145 beats rather than the 151 above. The maxim is that the aerobically fitter you become, the lower the pulse rate you need to work at to maintain this.

Anaerobic Threshold

As the speed of swimming, cycling or running increases and before the maximal oxygen uptake level has been attained, the anaerobic threshold is reached. This anaerobic threshold is marked by an increase in breathing rate and an increase in effort to maintain the same speed of swimming, cycling or running. Lactic acid is the by-product of anaerobic work and the breathing and effort effects are caused by the partial buffering or neutralising of this lactic acid. Although most energy is being provided by the aerobic system at this intensity, the amount of energy provided anaerobically gradually rises. Bicarbonate present in the bloodstream reacts with the lactic acid caused by this anaerobic work to produce carbon dioxide. It is this carbon dioxide which stimulates the increased respiration. Cyclists or runners will recognise when this anaerobic threshold is being reached by the difficulty which arises when they try to carry on a conversation. This is an easy way to monitor the level of the intensity of the training effect.

1. The anaerobic threshold can rise to about 80% or even more of the VO_2 max in the very fit athlete. It may be only half this in the unfit person.
2. The aerobic training zone is between the athlete's aerobic and anaerobic thresholds.
3. The anaerobic training zone lies between the athlete's anaerobic threshold and his maximal heart rate.
4. The aerobic system provides most of the energy required for training in the aerobic zone.
5. The anaerobic system provides an increasing amount of energy as the intensity of effort increases and moves into the anaerobic zone.

Lactic Acid

The amount of lactic acid circulating in the blood usually varies in individuals from 1 to 2 millimoles of lactate per litre of blood (1–2 mmol/l). There is a significant increase in this figure during aerobic exercise. As the intensity increases, the concentration of lactic acid will rise up to around 4 mmol/l to correspond to the anaerobic threshold. When the intensity goes up above the anaerobic threshold, the lactate levels can rise to around 25mmol/l.

At around 4 to 5mmol/l (the anaerobic threshold level) the optimal endurance training effect should take place if the training effort is maintained for twenty minutes or more. However some athletes will reach their anaerobic threshold as soon as the level reaches just above 2mmol/l and some not until a level of 7mmol/l.

Lactate values are a more accurate measure of adaptation to endurance training than are VO_2 max estimates, and improvements can be more easily observed.

Adaptation to Training

The purpose of endurance training is to encourage physiological changes to take place which will improve the triathlete's ability to produce and make use of energy.

Flat out sprint training with adequate ful recovery will promote changes in the analactic anaerobic energy system. This is of limited benefit to triathletes.

High quality repetitions with sufficient recovery time to allow lactate levels to fall below 6mmol/l will promote changes in the lactic anaerobic energy systems. The amount of recovery time allowed depends on the amount of repetitions, the length of the repetitions and the intensity of effort required.

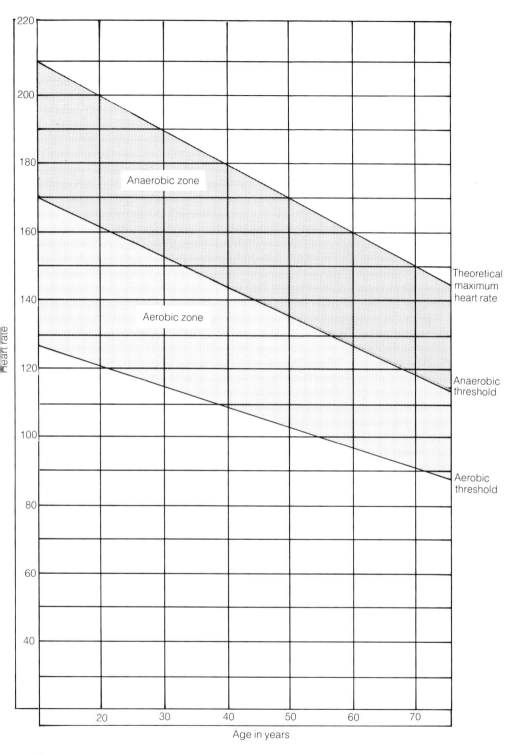

Fig 72   The graph gives an indication of aerobic and anaerobic training
          heart rates, as indicated by the Karvonen formula.

As the athlete's body adapts to aerobic training, the ability to transport oxygen to the muscles and to make use of that available oxygen improves. Endurance training increases the amount of blood that can be pumped from the heart with each beat, thus improving the heart's output. The training effect can be checked by a careful monitoring of the resting pulse. If the athlete falls into the habit of checking the resting pulse every morning before any training is done, he or she will find that it will fall over a period of time as the effects of training are felt. Total blood volume increases in response to training and with less viscosity, it flows more easily. The number of red blood cells and volume of haemoglobin also increases.

It may perhaps be relevant to note here that some endurance athletes have been diagnosed as anaemic. This is because some tests measure only the concentration of haemoglobin, and the increase in haemoglobin has not matched the increase in total blood volume.

More oxygen is made available within the muscle as the capillaries spreading through the working muscle increase in total number. The myoglobin, which take the oxygen from the bloodstream and pass it on to the mitochondria increase both in number and in size, making it easier to make use of the energy aerobically.

Fast and Slow Twitch Muscle Fibres

Slow twitch fibres – the red muscle fibres – are used for aerobic work.

Fast twitch fibres – the white muscle fibres – are used for anaerobic work.

The redness of the slow twitch fibres is due to the ready supply of blood needed to supply the oxygen for aerobic work. White fibres do not need blood to work anaerobically, so lacking blood, they are white.

Physiologists tell us that over a period of time with extensive endurance type training, some white fibres can be converted to red.

Aerobic training will lead to:

1. An improvement in an athlete's maximal oxygen.
2. An athlete's increased ability to hold back the onset of lactic acid build-up.
3. An increased percentage of VO_2 max at which the athlete can perform aerobically over a long period of time.
4. An increased ability to mobilise fats as a source of energy which is essential for competing in triathlon events of over two hours' duration.

PHYSIOLOGICAL IMPLICATIONS FOR THE FEMALE TRIATHLETE

In the short history of triathlon there has not been the prejudice shown against women competitors that has been evident in other sports' longer histories. For example, up until the 1968 Olympic games, a woman athlete was only allowed to compete in distances up to 800 metres on the running track and facilities for women athletes have often been sadly lacking compared to what is available for men.

However, the single most important limiting factor has been the attitude met by women wishing to take part in endurance training and events. This attitude has prevailed among sports spectators, but also among other women athletes and their advisers and coaches.

It is known that women can train as hard as men. There are anatomical and

Fig 73   Most men would be happy to finish in front of top woman, Cathy
Bow.

physiological differences and disadvantages which lead to the different performance levels.

Heart and Lungs

The woman's heart volume is approximately 25% less than in a man.

Blood Volume

The woman has 4–4·5l of blood compared to a man's 5–6l to transport the oxygen to the working muscles.

Red Cells

In women, oxygen carrying haemoglobin is 42% of the blood total compared to 47% in men. To transport 1l of oxygen, women have to use 9l of blood, while men only use 8 litres.

The Pelvis

A woman's wider pelvis lessens the mechanical efficiency of running, and to a lesser extent, cycling. The wider pelvis produces an exaggerated angle of the thigh bone bringing the knee closer into the centre.

Body Fat

A woman carries about 10% more body fat than a man. This body fat affects the maximum oxygen uptake by requiring oxygen without working in return. The extra supply of energy which may be available here does not compensate for this weight.

Sweating

Although women have a proportionatel equal amount of sweat glands to men, the lose heat less effectively. Consequently the efficiency of the working muscles i reduced as the blood is diverted to the ski to radiate away the heat that men are abl to lose by sweating more heavily, rathe than being used to transport oxygen.

Strength

Women have less muscle mass than men around 36% compared with around 42% o body weight in men. The strength levels ar lower by 55% to 80%.

Possible Amenorrhoea

The reduction of body fat often brough about by hard training can sometimes lead to periods stopping. If prolonged, thi could cause premature thinning of bone (osteoporosis) and also increase the risk o stress fractures resulting from reduced oestrogen levels.

Training Implications for Women

Women must spend the same amount o time in training as men if they wish to reacl the highest levels of competition. Th volume and intensity of training should b the same as for men and coaches must b prepared to work women as hard as men.

Iron and vitamin C supplements may b needed to offset the possibility of anaemia.

While there are differences in perform ance between men and women, it i interesting to read Great Britain's Directo of Athletic Coaching, Frank Dick, o women's athletics and training:

What we are at risk of doing is feeling that what we already know is all that we'll ever know. In Moscow they have an institute for the study of human potential and it is their job to look at new training methods to enhance that.

'You could say that could apply equally to men but we must understand that we could develop better training methods for the specific training of women than the ones we presently use . . . We're amassing a lot of information right now and I feel that women's performances will accelerate a lot faster than they are at the moment.' *(Athletics Weekly,* 29 July 1988)

If that can apply to one discipline of triathlon, what might be the implications for the other disciplines, and also applying it to cross and back-to-back training?

7 Developing a Programme

Planning a training programme for any sport is always difficult. If we were to look at just one aspect of triathlon, say running, we would need to build in training time for stamina, speed, strength, flexibility, sprinting, pace judgement, interval and repetition work and probably technique. A daunting task!

How much more daunting then to bring together three disciplines and look at not only a comprehensive programme for each of them but also the effects of each discipline's training on the other two. Equally important, of course is not just the hard work required, but also an adequate amount of time to rest and recover. It is little wonder that the world's best triathletes have long been full-time professionals.

It is never possible to outline a programme to be followed slavishly by every competitive triathlete, nor would it be welcomed by triathlon newcomers coming to the sport with a variety of athletic backgrounds and varying aims and objectives.

However, there are certain principles of development and training which apply to all triathletes and these do need to be considered when laying down annual programmes and planning the make-up of weekly and monthly schedules.

PRINCIPLES OF TRAINING

Overload

The training workload has to be sufficiently demanding so that it encourages the body to adapt and improve performance capacity. Both the amount and intensity of training in all three disciplines can be determined with this in mind.

Progression

The amount of training must gradually increase as the triathlete becomes fitter and more proficient and adapts to previous training loads. The amount of distance aerobic training will steadily increase during the off-season period and the quality of both the aerobic and anaerobic work will improve during the period leading up to the competitive season. Triathletes should be wary of trying to make too many increasing demands and improvements too quickly and should always consolidate their gains before moving on to the next phase. A short period of easy training is advisable before progressing to harder work.

Specificity

The effects of training are specific to the individual triathlete, the type of training being undertaken, and the particular discipline. Training must be geared to the individual triathlete if he or she is to gain

aximum benefit. The training load should
e related to the triathlete's present level of
ness and to his or her ability in each of the
ree disciplines.

echnique

hereas athletes in individual sports need
be technically proficient in just the one
ort, a triathlete needs to have excellent
chnique in three quite different activities.
e importance of putting much work into
arning a good technique – particularly in
e early, skill-seeking days – cannot be
eremphasised. It may be boring, time-
nsuming and energy sapping, but any
e spent on technique will be repaid over
d over again when things get tough in
ces.

est and Recovery

covery is an important part of the training
ogramme, for it is during the recovery
ase, after training is over, that adaptation
kes place. Many triathletes ignore this
portant point and pride themselves on
ntinuous hard work without ever taking a
eak, allowing insufficient recovery for
eir training schedules. As a result of this,
ey do not progress at the rate they would
e and suffer from overtraining symptoms.
As a general rule, running training is
ore stressful than cycling training, which
turn is more stressful than swimming
aining. Also, anaerobic training is more
ressful than aerobic training and requires
ore recovery between sessions. Cer-
inly, hard effort interval running training
ould not be undertaken more than twice
ach week and then only at certain times of
e annual training programme.
Many coaches in individual sports talk
out the concept of 'hard/easy' training

days or sessions. How hard is 'hard' and just
how easy is 'easy' depends entirely upon the
individual athlete. Beginners in any sport
often have little concept of how hard it is
possible to train when fitness has been won
over a period of years. Novice swimmers
would find it difficult to accept that their
struggling attempts at covering a thousand
metres would often be less than a third of the
distance done as a warm-up by an international swimmer before an important race.

The concept of rest and recovery has
important bearings on aerobic fitness
levels. Maximum heart rate is not a true or
accurate measure, rather it is how quickly
recovery takes place. As fitness improves,
so will the resting heart rate drop and
recovery become quicker. It is not unusual
for a fit athlete's heart rate to drop by a third
after maximum effort in less than a minute.
It is important to keep a record of your
resting pulse before exercise as this, as
well as recovery rate, is a good indicator of
improving fitness.

Reversibility

Unfortunately, as soon as training stops,
the improvements in performance which
have been gained, begin to reverse. The
rate at which improvements are lost is
generally similar to or quicker than that at
which they were gained. Triathletes who
have years of aerobic fitness in triathlon or
the single sports of swimming, cycling, or
running, will lose fitness far more slowly
than those who have only recently begun to
train for the sport.

Goal Setting

A comprehensive training programme will
prepare the triathlete for the races that he
or she selects. A great amount of thought

should be given both to races chosen, and to the number of races in which the triathlete wishes to compete during a season. It is important that whatever goals set are realistically attainable, but also sufficiently demanding to encourage the individual to train hard for success. Goals need not necessarily involve winning a race; finishing a particular distance or achieving split times in whatever discipline can be just as satisfying to the improver.

It can also be helpful for triathletes to set short-term goals to be achieved in training in any one week or month. By keeping a diary or log book, comparisons with previous weeks at the same time of year can easily be made and goals for the future set.

ANNUAL TRAINING PROGRAMME

Britain's unsuitable weather does not make competing in triathlon feasible as a year round objective. Even if it were possible, triathlete would be ill-advised to compete all year round. A long-term plan is required to give a training programme a sense of development and direction, with the training being geared for specific races at a specific time of year. In Britain, this main competition period would extend from May to September.

This is not to say that triathletes should not race during the off-season; it can be very enjoyable and a welcome mental break to take part in running, swimming or

Fig 74   On a hot day, any cooling effect is welcome.

MONTH	PERIOD	TRAINING WORK
December January February March (1st ½)	Preparation	Mainly aerobic base work
March (2nd ½) April May	Pre-competition	Aerobic and anaerobic, moving to specific fitness
June July August September	Competition	Work aimed at racing and competing well, including possible remedial work between races.
October November	Transition	Active rest

g 75   An annual training programme for a triathlete wishing to compete
during the summer in Great Britain.

ycling races, cross-country or cyclo-ross, biathlons or indoor swim triathlons utside the main competitive season; but 1ese races should fit into the training rogramme and become part of it, without 1e triathlete feeling the need to make pecial preparations for the competition. hese races should be used as more of a uide and indicator to the triathlete's grow-1g fitness.

A triathlete will wish to ensure that he or he is not let down in races by having one eak discipline. When deciding how to reak up the training time available, this 1ould be taken into consideration. If one vent is particularly strong, the time spent 1 this can perhaps be reduced until the vo other disciplines are approaching parity. riathletes without a running background 1ould beware that they do not overtrain on

running to begin with. It is the most demanding and physically taxing on the body's muscular and skeletal strength, and increases in demand must be gradual. Once comparable strengths in all three disciplines are attained, the triathlete must decide how best to share the training time to maintain this. Triathlon is time-consuming but good management can ensure that time is not wasted.

The annual training programme can be broken up into four periods which are not necessarily distinct from each other.

1.   Preparation Period

This takes place during the winter months from November through to March or April. This is the time for laying the base of aerobic work, working on technique and ironing out faults, ensuring that strength and mobility are developed. In short, this is a period of hard work to develop fitness which will give the triathlete the background to work from in the pre-competitive and competition phases.

2. Pre-competition Period

This is when the triathlete moves from the base work established into training to develop specific fitness required for racing. This period will contain both aerobic and anaerobic training. In Britain this would be over the months of March, April and May.

3. Competition Period

The training is aimed at preparing the triathlete for important competitions and for ensuring that any remedial steps needed can be fitted in between these races.

4. Transition Period

A period of active rest where the triathlete can recover from the effects of the competitive season and can even gently try his hand at other sports. This period would take place in October and the beginning of November before leading back into the preparation phase. Although this is a resting period, it is not advisable that the triathlete should do nothing at all during this time. Easy sessions to maintain some aerobic fitness are necessary, for, if not, the concept of reversibility comes into force.

At whatever period of the year, aerobic training should not be neglected. Triathlon is above all an endurance event, and an aerobic base must be maintained throughout.

TYPES OF TRAINING

If you train, you will progress.
If you train hard, you will progress mor quickly.
How you train will determine how quickl you progress.

There are many different ways to trair Even in triathlon's short history, severa different methods have been expounde as the 'only way' or the 'best way'. When w look back through the history of swimminç cycling or running, we are in a bette position to view triathlon training history a a microcosm of the other three activities. I truth, we are still searching for the ideal wa to train; and even when one triathlet believes he has found it, it will certainly nc suit everybody.

What we do have are tried and teste concepts from swimming, cycling and rur ning, and the experience gained fror athletes in these three sports from whic triathletes can learn. It is interesting to not that the British Miler's Club, an organisatio which is dedicated to the improvement c middle distance running standards in Grea Britain, and which has included such not ables as Steve Ovett and Sebastian Co amongst its number, has long propounde the theory of five pace running in traininç that of race distance; above and below rac distance; and then speed and endurance An examination of top class triathlete training schedules, particularly as outline by Dave Scott, would indicate that this kin of a specific mixture of training pace i already being used. Learning betwee sports never ends, and athletes who ar too shortsighted to regard other sports d themselves little favour.

Specific training for triathlon involve training in swimming, cycling and runninç rganised in one of the three following orms.

. *Continuous/Distance training.* A continuous swim, cycle or run completed at a steady pace. In cycling and running, this will be the aerobic base; after the entry level in swimming, it may not necessarily be so. Swimming incurs less stress generally in the body than running or cycling, and after the initial build-up when the novice is attempting merely to cover distance, it may well be that short rest repetition training maintains and builds aerobic conditioning better than swimming pure distance.

. *Mixed pace.* A continuous swim, cycle or run completed at a varying pace. The Swedish term, 'fartlek', meaning speed-play, is often used in conjunction with this type of training; more often in running than swimming or cycling.

. *Repetition/Interval type training.* Periods of swimming, cycling and running, interspersed with periods of rest.

Continuous Training

Medium and long-term aerobic work both involve training of a continuous form. The intensity of the training run, cycle or swim will decrease as the duration increases.

Of prime importance in undertaking a number of long training efforts is that they effectively mentally prepare the triathlete for taking part in a long distance event. The physical effects of such training sessions are:

. A development of the oxygen transport system and the triathlete's ability to perform prolonged activity at a high percentage of maximum oxygen uptake.

. An increase in the stroke volume of the heart.

3. A lowering of the resting pulse.

4. A conditioning of the triathlete to resist the fatigue of the race without straining the adaptation process. It is important that the pace of the training session is sufficiently easy that straining does not occur.

5. A utilisation of fats. With good aerobic fitness, the burning of fatty acids along with glycogen will start early on in a continuous swim, cycle or run. By burning the fatty acids, less glycogen is required, and is therefore conserved which will prevent the body from running out of energy earlier than otherwise.

However important continuous training is, it is not necessary to be always going out and trying to work up to mega-mileages. To attempt this would be to have the body constantly at a low ebb and open to potential injuries and stress.

Mixed Pace Training/Fartlek

It is possible to make continuous training more stressful (and less boring) by varying the pace and the difficulty of the course. Hills can be included to stress the triathlete and to take him closer to his VO_2 max. Course changes will not usually be possible in the swimming pool, however!

The fast and hard stages of the run, cycle or swim force the triathlete to approach his VO_2 max and induce a shortage of oxygen to the working muscles. This will often occur during races and the triathlete needs to be prepared for it. This oxygen debt is repaid during the less stressful stages of the training session. The periods during these sessions when there is a shortage of oxygen encourage adaptation of the aerobic system.

This fartlek type session could be beneficial to triathletes who are always finding it difficult to make sufficient time for training. It combines aerobic and anaerobic training but leaves the specific make-up of the session to the individual. It is possible to either structure a fartlek session by pre-determining the fast and slow sections of the course, or to leave speed open and just set the distance to be covered and wait until the individual triathlete decides for himself. This second option does require great self-discipline however. Fartlek training can easily be structured for a group with each triathlete in turn giving the signal to set out on the next fast section.

Repetition/Interval Type Training

The term 'repetition training' applies to training sessions which are aimed at developing the anaerobic system, while the term 'interval training' applies to sessions which are aimed at developing the aerobic system. However there is not an absolute distinction between the two and there will be an overlap between longer repetition sessions and shorter interval sessions where there will be a mixed training effect. To avoid confusion the term 'repetition training' will be used throughout.

It is important that a triathlete has a good idea of the speed he or she is aiming to maintain during a race. Experienced triathletes will be able to use the previous season's efforts as a guide, while triathletes with less experience should do a specific time trial – not as far as the total race distance – in all three disciplines so that they have a working target to aim for. Races or time trials in the three sports, particularly during the non-competitive season, are a good indication as to fitness and to how training is progressing.

Repetition training requires repeated

efforts interspersed with periods of recover these recovery periods can be either active (easy swimming, cycling or jogging between the efforts) or passive (resting).

However, not all repetition type trainin sessions will promote the same effect an the number of variables which can be use to create different training loads and effect of training are:

1. The distance and duration of eac repetition.
2. The speed and intensity of each repe tion.
3. The total number of repetitions an sets of repetitions.
4. The recovery period.
5. The type of recovery – active or passive
6. The course (in cycling and running least) over which the repetitions take place

This repetition type training can be su divided into four categories – three large anaerobic and one largely aerobic although there are aspects of both in thre of the four types.

1. Speed work (this type of training purely anaerobic).
2. Short duration/short to medium recove work.
3. Long duration/medium to short recove work.
4. Anaerobic threshold work.

Speed Work

Flat out efforts in the three disciplines whic last for under half a minute will develo pure speed, and also speed endurance. full recovery should be allowed betwee efforts.

Some triathletes decide that they wou be more gainfully training by developin

Fig 76   Short bursts of flat out effort are sometimes needed to get away
from chasing cyclists . . .

Fig 77   . . . or to be in a good position to start the swim.

endurance rather than pure speed; and while this may well be so to some extent, there are bound to be occasions when competing – trying to outsprint a rival at the end of the run section or needing to get into a tight bike turn first with space only for one rider, for example – that require absolute speed.

Short Duration/Short to Medium Recovery

Time taken for training effort, up to two minutes.
Time taken for rest (for two minutes effort): two minutes in swimming; three to five minutes in cycling; five to seven minutes in running.

An adequate recovery is important as the effort required is approaching one hundred per cent. An active rest is better than a passive rest with easy jogging between running repetitions and low gear spinning on cycling repetitions.

This is an extremely fatiguing type of training which exercises both the aerobic and anaerobic systems equally, and adapts the body to accept a high level of lactic acid and oxygen debt. This is crucial for races when an extra turn of speed and effort is required to attack a hill when cycling or running or to burst out of a tight swimming pack which is slowing you down and inhibiting your stroke.

Typical swimming session (for an eleven minute, eight hundred metres pace swimmer). Six repeats of one hundred and fifty metres in two minutes, going every four minutes.
In training shorthand, this would be written: 6 x 150m in 2 mins, 4 mins swim and rest (or going every 4 mins).

Typical cycling session (for a fourteen mile per hour pace cyclist – roughly twenty-five miles in an hour and three-quarters).
Six repeats of half a mile in two minutes with an easy cycle back to the starting point in four minutes.
In shorthand: 6 x 800m in 2 mins, 6 min cycle and rest (or going every 6 mins).

Typical running session (for a six-minute mile pace runner).
Six repeats of six hundred metres in two minutes fifteen seconds, with a jog recover of six minutes forty five seconds in between, sufficient to cover six to eight hundred metres.
In shorthand: 6 x 600m in 2.15, going every 9 mins.

As training and fitness progress, improvements can be made by:

1. Speeding up effort.
2. Reducing recovery time.
3. Increasing number of repetitions.

It would be expected that speed would increase into the competitive season.

Long Duration/Medium to Short Recovery

This is sometimes known as VO_2 max type training.

VO_2 max is the amount of oxygen, measured in litres, that can be utilised in one minute. To compare between individuals this is expressed in millilitres of oxygen utilised per minute per kilogram of body weight. (By losing weight, an increase in VO_2 max will occur automatically.) It is important to develop the VO_2, even though it is not the be-all and end-all of athletic capability.

It is interesting to read what Dr Clyde Williams wrote of top British triathlete and Great Britain team member Bernie Shrosbree with a VO_2 max of 78, in 1980:

'If a common training speed was chosen for the whole group then B. Shrosbree would be far less stretched than his team-mates. Conversely, if the training pace was set according to the capacity of B. Shrosbree then the intensity would be too high for the rest of the group.'

At the time of writing, Bernie had not even taken part in a triathlon, his sport was biathlon and cross-country skiing. However one of the reasons that he was able to make a relatively easy transition to another endurance sport was his high VO_2 max. Theoretically, at any given pace Bernie would be able to sustain his effort for a longer time than someone with a lower VO_2 max. For any triathlete, training to raise the VO_2 max means being able to race closer to the aerobic capacity.

Time taken for the training effort, from two minutes up to six minutes, as fitness increases, occasionally up to ten minutes which will be repeated two or three times. Before a triathlete gains sufficient fitness, it may be necessary to break the efforts into smaller sections with a very short rest interval between. It is important in this type of training to work at a high intensity by elevating the heart rate early in the effort and then maintaining it.

Typical swimming session (for our eleven minute, eight hundred metre pace swimmer). Four repeats of one hundred metres in ninety seconds, with ten seconds break between. The set to be done three times with a three minute recovery period between sets.

In shorthand: 3 sets of 4 x 100m in 90, 10 secs rest. 3 mins between sets.

Typical cycling session (for our fourteen mile per hour cyclist).
Five repeats of one mile in five minutes with an easy cycle of one minute in between. After the five repetitions, an active rest of five minutes is taken before the set is repeated.
In shorthand: 2 sets of 5 x 1 mile in 5 mins, going every 6 mins. 5 mins between sets.

Typical running session (for our six minute mile pace runner).
Five repeats of eight hundred metres in three minutes and thirty seconds with a minute and a half recovery in between. This would be an extremely fatiguing training session and it would be unlikely that this length of run repetition would be able to be repeated other than by the extremely fit triathlete who has built up his running strengths over a long period.
In shorthand: 5 x 800m in 3.30, 90 secs rest.

Anaerobic Threshold

This is sometimes referred to as *Gerschler type interval work*. The feature of this type of training is a large number of repetitions with only a short recovery time between. The aim is to elevate the anaerobic threshold so that a higher work rate can be maintained throughout the race. There are many examples of top class endurance athletes whose VO_2 max is not particularly high, but who are able to maintain a higher percentage of that figure for a long period of time.

Typical swimming session (for our eleven minute pace eight hundred metres swimmer).

Twenty repetitions of fifty metres in forty seconds, with ten seconds break in between.
In shorthand: 20 x 50m in 40 secs, going every 50 secs.

Typical cycling session (for our fourteen mile per hour cyclist).
Ten repetition efforts each lasting one minute with thirty seconds easy cycling recovery in between.
In shorthand: 10 x 1 min, going every 90 secs.

Typical running session (for our six minute miler).
Fifteen repetitions of two hundred metres in forty seconds with a forty seconds jog recovery in between.
In shorthand: 15 x 200m in 40 secs, 40 secs jog rec.

It should be remembered that one of the principles of training is progression, and this applies to all our different types of sessions. As the triathlete becomes fitter, progression in our repetition training sessions could include:

1. Increasing the speed of each repetition;
2. Increasing the distance in each repetition effort;
3. Increasing the number of repetitions;
4. Increasing the number of sets;
5. Decreasing the amount of rest taken.

Any training session may also include more than one type of training, both to vary the session and also to work on the different training effects. In swimming particularly, with its quicker recovery period it is possible to include an example of all types of training within an hour's session time.

Which Type of Sessions? Which Time of Year?

Within our four divisions of the annual training programme, there are shifts of emphasis as to the type of session which should make up the bulk of the work at any one time. However, a rigid division is not advisable as all the training effects need to be maintained to some extent, and in addition, injury can be more likely to occur if an athlete moves from, say, endurance work to speed type training. It is far better to have a variety of all kinds of training throughout the year, even though there will be a main purpose for each phase.

1. *Preparation Period*

During this time there will be a gradual increase in the training mileage, levelling out towards the end of the period. Training will comprise a mixture of aerobic and anaerobic work, although the main emphasis will be on the development of aerobic endurance. A triathlete would wish to include:

1. Long runs (ten miles or more) and long cycle rides (forty miles or more), at an easy pace;
2. Medium length runs and rides at faster pace;
3. Aerobic type swimming sessions although not always necessarily pure distance;
4. Fartlek work in all three sports;
5. Some repetition training sessions geared more towards aerobic work than anaerobic type work, although not exclusively;
6. Work on technique in all three disciplines;
7. Mobility and strength work;

6. Races and time trials in the three sports, perhaps at longer distances.

2. Pre-competition Period

As the year moves towards the competitive season, the emphasis will move towards the specific fitness required for triathlon racing. The total mileage covered will reduce gradually as the quality of the training improves. There will be a move away from an aerobic emphasis towards anaerobic, although the aerobic base must be maintained throughout the year. A triathlete would wish to include:

1. Long runs and rides, although less than during the preparation phase;
2. An increase of the medium length runs and rides, moving towards race pace;
3. Aerobic and anaerobic type swimming sessions;
4. An increase in repetition training sessions with the emphasis now towards anaerobic work;
5. A maintenance of technique, mobility and strength work;
6. Some outdoor swimming work if possible;

7. Pressure sessions, still possibly in the form of races in individual disciplines with the athlete working hard throughout;
8. Specific work on weaknesses.

3. Competition Period

A maintenance of general and specific fitness already gained, and a preparation of the triathlete for racing. The content of each training session will be governed by the racing programme (and any travelling involved) but will taper towards the race. Much of the aerobic work will now be taken care of by racing, although if there is a considerable gap between races, the triathlete should still maintain the aerobic base within a training session.

4. Transition Period

Some training must be maintained although it is the ideal time for the triathlete to try different sports. The amount of training is both low and low key; the triathlete should arrive at the preparation phase keen to start back on steady, hard work.

8 Racing: Preparation, Diet and Equipment

RACE PREPARATION

Planning for a race does not start just minutes or hours before the gun sounds on race day! Rather it goes back the weeks, months and years of training, learning and gaining experience. The last few days and hours are vital in bringing together all the pre-learned knowledge and ensuring that it

Fig 78   Concentration is required before a race.

doesn't go to waste by panicky, last-minute wrong decisions and incorrect preparation.

Tapering

In all sports, tapering for a race is an art in itself. The experience gained over the years by millions of competitors, research by coaches and the effects in races of different types of tapering has led to certain basic tenets. The rule of thumb goes something like, 'reduce the amount of training before a race'. That statement is all-embracing, and while it may be used as a starting-point, it is of little specific help to the novice triathlete who needs to know how much and for how long before an event the workload should be reduced. As triathletes become more experienced, they are able to call on their own reserves of knowledge of previous races entered and to look back in training diaries to see what was done in the few days before the race. From there it is a simple step to tie up the kind of race and the feelings experienced during it: whether things went wrong or right; whether tiredness was felt early on or not; if any discipline was particularly hard or even if it was one of those magic days when you are competing at your absolute peak and carried along on a kind of euphoria through the race.

It is important that the triathlete does not go into the race absolutely shattered from hard training right up to the day before the race and certainly no one should attempt to

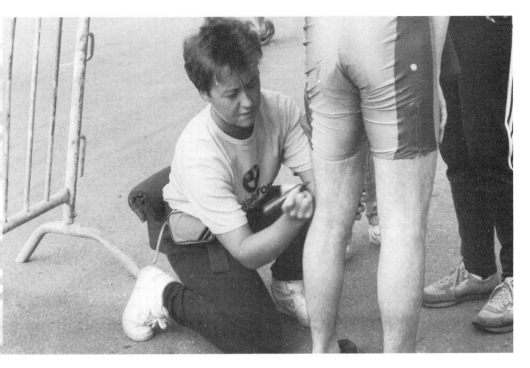

Figs 79–81   Marking of the arms and legs is a pre-race ritual for triathlon.

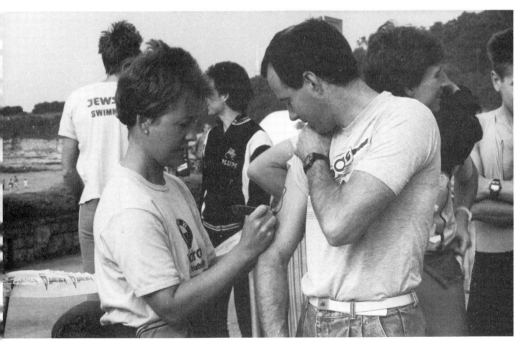

Fig 80

97

Fig 81

increase the intensity of training sessions in the last ten days leading up to the event. Equally, starting to taper by doing less training too early can lead to a fall-off in fitness.

Some runners and their coaches have experimented with the 'ten day effect' taper. Full recovery from an extremely hard interval type running session can take up to ten days, at which time there seems to be a gain in strength from that session; so a demanding training session is undertaken a week and a half before race day and light training is maintained in the intervening period. Great confidence is needed by the athlete while he or she is tired to be sure that he or she will feel fully recovered and strong on the race day.

As running is the most physically demanding sport in triathlon and needs the most recovery, special care must be taken that no hard interval sessions are planned too near to race day. As recovery from swimming is usually fairly rapid amongst competent triathletes, fairly hard work can be maintained nearer to the big day. With three or four days to go, the athlete should listen to his or her body and plan rest or training accordingly. Absolute rest the day before the race is not always a good idea as muscles can get tight, restlessness can set in by sitting around, and there can be a feeling of bloatedness from having done nothing when your body is normally busy racing around and burning off all the calories consumed. If you feel that you do need a day off completely, it may be better to take it two days before the race rather than the day before.

Triathlon does not yet have a long history and the sport has very few experienced coaches. It would be fair to say that the art and science of tapering for a triathlon race is very much an unknown medium. A well-planned taper allows the competitor to go into the race rested and eager to put himself on the line, willing to try to race all-out and find out if his strengths or weaknesses are going to have the upper hand. There are no hard and fast rules, each individual must experiment and see what works best for him or her and regulate the tapering period accordingly.

There are perhaps more variable factors to be experienced in a triathlon event than in any other sport and this, in itself, makes the preparations for racing an integral and fascinating part of the sport.

Winning your own Race

If success is to be judged on winning and losing alone, then 99% of triathletes are failures! Only one athlete in each age and sex category can come first, and there are many other factors which an athlete should use to judge his own successes.

Have I done better in this race than last year? If not, has injury or a break in training been the reason why?
Have I beaten, or been beaten by other competitors who usually finish near me in a race?

Fig 82   Patrick Barnes works as hard as any winner to finish his races.

Is this my type of race? Does the weather and terrain on the swimming/cycling/running sections suit my strengths or weaknesses? Don't use these explanations as an excuse for poor performance, though.

Has my training been consistent or poor?

Have I raced as well as I could have expected, given my training programme?

Have other things outside the sport played a part in my performance?

Have I tried as hard as I could, and given everything, or have I 'backed off'?

Even when things do go wrong in a race, it is useful to evaluate it. There is only rarely such a thing as 'just one of those bad races'. There is often a reason for a poor performance.

Racing can be a useful exercise for when an athlete is unfit or coming back afte injury. Specific aims can be set within the race, to attempt one of the disciplines fla out, to use the race as a fartlek traininç session, or just to get used to the 'hurt' Most triathletes favour one discipline anc secretly (or otherwise) regard it as thei strength, look forward to it in the race anc set out to pass as many athletes as possi ble on this phase.

The Course

If it is at all possible, try to go over the course before the race starts, even if you have to arrive early in the morning to dc this.

Be prepared early with all kit, equipment and bike. Know how you will set it all out ir

Fig 83   Rick Morris saves valuable seconds by starting to cycle before he has put his feet into the cycling shoes.

Fig 84   The author stoops down to fasten pedal straps.

the transition area; actually put it out at home and change clothing. Look out for any snags and decide what order you will put your clothes on in transition. Can you put some on when you're on the bike or starting the run?

Check the turning buoys in the swim section. Where is the best starting place? Is there something large to focus on for each leg of the swim? Are there special arrangements for coming out of the water into transition; is there a one way system there?

Check out the climbs and descents on the bike course. Do you need to change your gearing? Is there a prevailing wind? Is the road surface good or poor? Are there any dangerous corners? Are there any places where it is easy to go off course? Have an idea of the mileage at certain parts of the course. Check for any landmarks to

remind you of a particularly tough section coming up.

Go over the course map and race instructions that the organiser has supplied. Where are the water stations? Will I need to take food? Can a friend supply me with food or water, or would I be disqualified if I took it? How close can I get to the racecourse on raceday? Is parking easy or difficult? How much time do I need to get there?

Assume that the race start is fifteen minutes before the programme says it is, as time just slides away in the minutes before a race. You'll need the extra time to go to the toilet one more time, to repair sunglasses, to borrow a swimhat when yours splits, to tie another elastic together, to chase after your number when it blows away, to sit down and do a few easy stretches and to prepare yourself mentally

Fig 85 *You may want to take all this for a race . . .*

Fig 86 *. . . or just this!*

Fig 87   Transitions will be made easier and faster by having velcro fasteners (cycle shoes) or toggles (running shoes).

for the race ahead. Don't panic. Everybody is nervous before the race starts, however good or experienced they are. Be determined to have the best possible race that you can, to work on your strengths and to minimise the time losses on your weaknesses. You are here because you have chosen to be, because you're a triathlete.

When you cross the finish line, in whatever position, you've won. You've beaten that temptation that told you to drop out or ease off when the going got tough. Now pamper yourself, warm down easily, walk or jog around, try to stretch gently. Drink water and eat something easily digestible like fruit. Put a tracksuit on if it's at all cold, talk to your friends about the race and start planning for the next one.

DIET AND NUTRITION

For the athlete, food is a fuel. Just as a car engine requires petrol, so the athlete requires food.

In sporting history there have been many weird and wonderful diets, with athletes of all kinds looking for the miracle food that will make them go faster. Well, there isn't one, but sensible eating will enable you to make full use of your training whilst an inappropriate diet will only detract from your potential performance. The quality of all calories in food is not equal, and the 'human dustbin' myth which propounded that it didn't matter what you ate because it would all be burnt up, is happily exploded. However, even with our knowledge of dietary

Fig 88   Finishing the event is everything.

requirements, some athletes are notorious for their eating habits, their ability to eat junk food and still compete at top level. One has to question how much better they might compete with an optimum diet, and what is the likely long-term effect on their performance and health?

Health and Fitness

Sensible eating for triathlon performance and training is also sensible eating for good health. The nutrients in food that are required for both the triathlete and the non-triathlete are:

1. *Carbohydrate*. The main supply of energy to the body.
2. *Fats*. A stored source of energy and an absorber of vitamins A, D, E, and K.
3. *Protein*. This is essential for repair and growth of body tissue.
4. *Vitamins and Minerals*. These are essential for the metabolism of the body.
5. *Water*. Many people, athletes and otherwise do not drink enough water. Over sixty per cent of the body is water and it needs to be replaced regularly.
6. *Fibre*. This is essential in the diet for the well-being of the digestive system.

A diet that is low in fat, sugar and concentrated protein, and high in complex carbohydrates reduces the highs and lows of energy levels in the body and increases the most immediate source of fuel for endurance events.

The benefits to health from this type of diet are enormous; by lowering the amount of fats and sugar, the cholesterol level is reduced which decreases the possibility of heart attacks. By eating less fat, it is easier to lose excess weight.

Protein, Fat and Carbohydrate

Carbohydrate contains 4 kcal/g.
Protein contains 9 kcal/g.
Fat contains 9 kcal/g.

Anybody taking in an excess of calories will gain weight. By reducing the intake of fat, it is possible to increase the intake of food containing carbohydrate or protein and maintain the same weight. As carbohydrate is the first fuel to be used to produce energy, it makes good sense for the active triathlete to increase the intake of carbohydrates.

The body is made up of *protein* and a regular intake of protein is needed to maintain the growth of body tissue. In the last resort it can be used as a fuel after all the carbohydrate and fat stores have been exhausted.

For the rebuilding of muscle tissue after exercise, the body is only able to use a little less than one gram of protein for each kilogram of body weight. For a 70kg (11 stone) male triathlete, this would work out at 60–70g of protein each day, 240–280 calories. A triathlete in an extremely hard period of training might increase this slightly to rebuild muscle tissue. However taking in too much protein will merely lead to the excess being excreted.

Fat in the diet has recently been blamed as the cause of high cholesterol levels and heart attacks, so cutting out fats from the diet might seem to be the ideal thing to do. However, it is an excess of fats that brings problems and some fat is necessary in the diet as;

a stored source of energy;
an aid to the absorption of vitamins A, D, E, and K;

a protector of vital organs; and a provider of bodily insulation.

The average non-athletic person in Great Britain eats as much as forty per cent of their daily food intake as fats and in America, it has been shown to be even more. Fat intake should be reduced to half of this forty per cent total, to around twenty per cent or less. Fats come in two forms, saturated and unsaturated (unsaturated fats are divided into monounsaturated and polyunsaturated). Examples of foods containing saturated fats include cheese, butter and cream, meat, chocolate and egg yolk. Monounsaturated fats include peanuts, cashew nuts and olives, while polyunsaturated fats will include vegetable oils, some nuts and fish. As a general rule, the poly-unsaturated fats (vegetable fats) are preferable to saturated fats (animal fats) fo good health.

A major benefit of being a triathlete is tha aerobic exercise increases the likelihood o excessive cholesterol (a cause of hear attacks) breaking away from the artery walls and being broken down in the liver.

Carbohydrate is the prime source o energy for endurance events and shoulc be a major part of the food intake. Fa comes in as an energy source later on ir the event. Carbohydrate comes in the form of sugar or starch. Starch in the form of fruit vegetables, pasta, bread and grains is tc be preferred to sugar as it provides both bulk, which slows the release of sugar intc the bloodstream and a steady energy level with vitamins and minerals.

Fig 89   This triathlete prefers to eat on the bike.

As much as seventy per cent of the food intake should be in the form of carbohydrates for the triathlete.

Vitamins and *minerals* are essential to allow our bodies to function properly. They help the processes which regulate metabolism, release energy and repair tissue.

Triathletes often ask whether supplements of vitamins are necessary. The easy reply is only if there is not an adequate supply in the triathlete's diet. Some dieticians recommend a supplement of vitamins B and C for the endurance athlete and if vitamin C is taken, this may often be in conjunction with iron which is not easily assimilated by the body on its own.

It is impossible to survive for long without *water*! The body requires a regular supply to function normally. It carries nutrients and regulates body temperature. Too much water loss, particularly during long races and in hot conditions leads to dehydration which prevents the body from working effectively and can lead to sad sights at the end of long races when – to misquote Kipling – the body is required:

To serve its turn long after it is gone,
And so hold on when there is nothing in it
Except the Will which says to it: "Hold on!"

Triathletes must drink lots of water, particularly in long races and under hot conditions.

Fibre is essential to ensure the proper health of our digestive system. In our present society, the appearance of food is a valuable marketing tool and many highly processed foods have had a large proportion of the fibre removed. To overcome this, it is necessary to include foods such as wholemeal bread in the diet.

The Triathlete's Diet

The seven essential nutrients and the types of food which provide them have been discussed above. How best to combine them is the next step in trying to detail a suitable diet for the triathlete. We have already seen that many sedentary people have an unhealthy diet, and many inexperienced triathletes have similar eating habits. A change should be made to include a different proportion of proteins, fats and carbohydrates in the diet.

1. Increase carbohydrate intake to sixty per cent or more of total intake.
2. Reduce fat intake to twenty per cent or less of total intake.
3. Maintain or reduce protein intake to ten per cent of total intake.

These figures are, of necessity, guides only. Many world class triathletes have over seventy per cent of carbohydrates in their dietary intake.

To approach these guidelines, triathletes may have to do the following.

1. Try to choose a diet with a variety of foods.
2. Increase carbohydrate intake to sixty per cent or more of total.
3. Reduce intake of sugar.
4. Reduce intake of fat to twenty per cent or less of total.
5. Attempt to eat polyunsaturated rather than saturated fats (marked on cooking oils and margarines as high in polyunsaturates). Eat less eggs. If you eat red meat, choose the leaner cuts and trim off excess fat. Eat more chicken and fish rather than red meat.
6. Reduce cholesterol intake to a minimum.
7. Reduce added salt (both put on food or used in cooking) intake.

8. Increase intake of cereals, fruit, vegetables, bread, rice, beans and pasta.
9. Grill food rather than fry it.
10. Use skimmed or semi-skimmed milk rather than whole milk.
11. Cut down on or cut out cakes, puddings, biscuits, sweets.
12. Cut out high calorie fizzy drinks.

Race Food

If the triathlete's diet has sufficient carbohydrates, there is little point in changing it radically before a competition. The idea of carbo-loading as used by some endurance athletes, especially marathon runners, where the body is drained of carbohydrates a week before the event and then saturated with them three days before the race, is losing favour. A high carbohydrate diet should be maintained.

During the race, even over the shorter distances, many triathletes will drink. If food is needed, fruit is easily digestible and the effects are felt fairly quickly, usually within ten minutes. It is important to experiment before the race to anticipate when food will be needed and take it before feeling depleted.

After the race, the glycogen stores in the body will be depleted, so it makes good sense to eat soon after crossing the finishing line and replenish the stores by eating an adequate amount of carbohydrate and also some protein, vitamins and minerals.

CLOTHING

One of the attractions of triathlon competition is undoubtedly the clothing. Racedays are often as much a fashion parade as an athletic event with the transition area containing the models and mannequins. However, there is nothing in the rule book to say that comfortable clothing has to be unattractive, and triathlon suffers less than most sports with rules and regulations governing what may and may not be worn.

In many respects, clothing has evolved along with the sport and while many triathletes still prefer to compete in the specific clothing for each discipline, taking time out in transition to change from swimming to cycling to running clothing; others prefer to race in a trisuit or a variety of different combinations of clothing from triathlon's three component parts.

Comfort and efficiency are the keywords.

Swimming Costume

As well as for swimming, many triathletes are choosing to complete the entire triathlon race wearing a costume. It is well to remember that racing trunks or costumes are intended to be very close fitting to avoid any drag during the pool-based swimming races and may become uncomfortable if worn for a period of two hours or more. Try out the costume in training before wearing it for a race.

Goggles

Goggles help you to see, and during pool training they stop your eyes from weeping from prolonged immersion in water containing chlorine and lime. It is essential that the goggles are clean, watertight and comfortable as there is nothing more frustrating than having to tread water in the middle of a race to adjust your goggles while everyone else is swimming past you.

Swim Cap

In cold water this will do much to prevent body heat escaping from the head. Wear two rubber hats or a neoprene one in severe conditions. Most race organisers supply a brightly coloured hat which must be worn over the top of your own if you are wearing two.

Wetsuit

The wetsuit will keep you protected from the worst of the cold water and will also provide some buoyancy. Present regulations in Great Britain restrict the thickness of the wetsuit to 5mm, although some imported from abroad contravene these regulations. The wetsuit should be close-fitting, although not so close as to restrict movement; care should be taken when trying out a suit to check that it will not cause soreness or chafing around the neck or underarms. A little grease applied to these and other pressure points may be worth considering. Despite the wetsuit's warming properties, the hands and fingers will undoubtedly be cold when the triathlete arrives in the swim/cycle transition area, and it is important that the wetsuit can be easily removed even when the hands are numbed with cold. Make sure that all the zips and velcro fasteners are easily accessible.

Cycling Shoes

All good cycling shoes can be locked into the pedals, either by the traditional method of raised shoe plates with a slot for the back pedal edge to fit into or by one of the new shoe systems manufactured by, for example, Look, Adidas Systeme 3, or Aero. It matters little which system is used, as long as the shoe is securely fixed so that all the power exerted by the legs is transmitted through to the wheels. Many triathletes leave their shoes locked into the pedals in the transition area and start to pedal with their bare feet on top of the shoes in order to save a few valuable seconds on the cycle stage. Extra time can be saved by the use of velcro or straps for tying the shoes rather than laces.

Cycling Shorts

Cycling shorts are cut long on the leg to avoid chafing. They are normally made from lycra or a lycra type material and have a padded crotch (usually chamois, but sometimes a lighter, thinner material) to add some comfort and avoid the worst of the soreness during the ride.

Cycling Top

Cycling tops seem to be worn less and less for races as triathletes seem happy to wear a vest, t-shirt or trisuit. However, for the longer events the back pockets of a cycle jersey can be extremely valuable for carrying a banana or a wholefood crunchy bar to stave off the hunger knock.

Cycling Mitts

These cut off gloves are padded on the palm and around the inside of the thumb to give a more comfortable grip and some protection against shock and numbness. They are also handy for touching off any pieces of grit which may get stuck on the front wheel. Mitts might seem to be a luxury, but on a longer ride they give much comfort and protection.

Cycle Helmet

These are compulsory for competition. Hardshell or hairnet types are permitted for racing at the moment, although it seems likely that BTA legislation in the near future will more closely govern the type of protection given by helmets. Aerodynamic helmets with a hard plastic or fibre-glass outer coating are popular, and there are adaptations taking place which will maintain the teardrop shape while affording the protection presently given by the hardshell type.

Sunglasses

Although 'shades' might seem a luxury, they are welcomed in a long race to cut down on glare and avoid squinting. They also help to lessen tension around the face and neck.

Running Shoes

The suitability of footwear was discussed earlier in Chapter 4 on 'Running'. To reiterate, triathletes should look for comfort, padding, cushioning and protection. Avoidance of injury is a must and the downthrust of body weight on to one foot when running is considerable. Some triathletes who always find they have a running injury or continually sore leg muscles may need to wear an orthotic to correct an imbalance. These are expensive and it is little use buying one off the shelf. They should be fitted and moulded by an expert. Running shop staff, physiotherapy clinics or athletes' clinics in some hospitals may be able to help with advice as to where to seek guidance.

Socks

Putting socks on before either cycling or running takes time, but they are a protection against blisters and do give some extra protection and padding. If triathletes find that their feet are always stiff and solid after a cycling discipline, it may be worthwhile experimenting with leaving socks off. The small extra space allowed may stop constriction.

Running Shorts

Light, comfortable shorts with pants sown in are advisable. Don't wear new shorts for a race as the edges may cut and rub. Never wear shorts that are too tight or restricting for the same reason.

Running Vest

Should be light and comfortable. Nylon vests may feel sticky and rub and the benefit of their lightness may be out weighed by the comfort of cotton. Greasing under the arms and on the nipples before an event starts can help to avoid discomfort. In extreme cases, it may be worth putting elastoplasts over the nipples.

Hat or Cap

To avoid the worst of the sun on a hot day and to shade the eyes from glare when running, a hat is invaluable. A long brim will give extra protection over the front of the face, especially the nose.

Trishorts

Trishorts are very similar to cycling shorts but have less or no crotch padding. They are intended for use in all three disciplines.

Fig 90   Organised chaos at the end of many triathlons.

Trisuit

When the trisuit first appeared, it was greeted as the saviour of wasted transition time. Triathletes were able to wear the same piece of clothing for all three disciplines. A great many triathletes still wear this as the normal racing clothing. However, some did find the tightness of the suit too inhibiting on the run, and feel the lycra material doesn't let the skin 'breathe', but with competition becoming more intense and with only seconds separating the top finishers, the time saved in transition can mean the difference between winning or not. If the same clothing is worn for all three disciplines, care has to be taken with fixing on race numbers, either by having one on front and back, or by fixing the number to a thick elastic band or strap which is then put around the waist and can be turned to display the number on the back for the cycling section, or on the front for the run.

Tracksuits, Sweatshirts, Sweatpants

It is important to be warm before and after a race. Whether a triathlete chooses to wear the latest designer tracksuit or to throw on a well-worn jersey and baggy bottoms doesn't matter in the slightest. Warmth and comfort are the criteria.

Appendix

BTA Competition Rules

The following rules shall apply to all events sanctioned by the Association. Any promoter seeking variances of these rules must apply in writing for dispensation and all event literature shall clearly state any such variance.

1 Promoters

1.1 All persons staging an event shall comply with all aspects of the current *Organising and Staging a Triathlon* booklet issued by the Association.

1.2 Promoters of all events run under the rules of the Association must apply for a 'letter of sanction' from the Association.

1.3 All sanctioned events must be covered by insurance acceptable to the Association.

1.4 Only sanctioned events may qualify for cover under the Association's Event Insurance Policy.

1.5 All persons unable to produce a current race licence, issued by the Association, at time of registration shall pay the current levy. Payment of the levy does *not* entitle a competitor to any form of personal cover, as is available to holders of the race licence.

1.6 A complete list of all persons entered in an event shall be available at time of registration.

1.7 A provisional results sheet containing names and times of competitors shall be displayed at the presentation ceremony.

1.8 A ratified results list shall be despatched to all persons who registered in an event, with a copy being forwarded to the Association, no later than thirty days after the competition. The ratified results list shall give details of time, position and any category status. Wherever possible split times shall be given.

2 Swimming

2.1 The start signal shall be both audible and visible.

2.2 Competitors shall use no aids to swimming other than cap, goggles and costume. A costume may consist of a wetsuit, providing that the hands and feet are not covered, and the total thickness of the material (or materials) worn is no more than 5mm thick.

2.3 Competitors may stand during the race but shall not make progress along the course during this time other than is deemed necessary to execute entry into

and exit from the designated swimming course. I shallow waters, an exact point when swimming mus commence and may cease shall be appointed an marked.

2.4 Competitors shall, at all times, swim so that the do not deliberately obstruct or interfere with othe competitors. Making contact other than by acciden shall be declared unsporting impedence.

2.5 All swimming sections shall have a time limit. Th time limit will be specified on the briefing sheet an also given at the final briefing meeting. No safet cover shall leave the course, or be withdrawn unt instructed to do so by the safety officer.

2.6 At the end of the time limit any competitor still i the water shall be ordered to retire – at the discretio of the event referee.

2.7 All competitors shall wear a brightly coloure swim cap.

2.8 Competitors shall have their competition num bers clearly marked on their swimming cap and on th back of one or both hands.

2.9 No competitor will be allowed to continue unt their competition number has been recorded at th exit point.

2.10 No competitor shall be permitted to continu who, in the opinion of a race official, is unfit to do so.

3 Safety Provision – Swimming Section

3.1 Straight-line courses over 1.5km. On suc courses every competitor shall be accompanie individually by a safety craft.

3.2 Straight-line courses under 1.5km. Safety craft c platforms shall be stationed at 100m intervals alon the course, spaced from the back marker to 20 metres in front of the lead swimmer. Additional boat canoes shall patrol the swimming area to ensure tha no swimmer is at any time more than 50 metres fron safety cover.

3.3 Circuit courses. There should be spaced safet craft at 100m intervals with canoe, boat or lifeguar back-up so as to achieve a ratio of one safety unit pe 20 swimmers. At no time should any swimmer be mor than 50m from a safety unit, even when craft ar already engaged on recovery work.

3.4 A suitable craft shall act as a guide by maintain

ng station some 25 metres ahead of the leading male
and female competitors.

3.5   All turns shall be clearly marked by buoys or
other forms of marking, these being clearly visible to
the competitors.

3.6   The course shall be clearly marked every 50m
with a buoy or other marking device. Marker buoys
must be of a different colour from race hats.

4   Medical Cover

4.1   At all championships a qualified medical prac-
titioner is to be present.

4.2   First aid units in attendance are to be briefed by
the medical officer on the requirements of treatment
for shock and cold.

4.3   Sufficient blankets are to be on hand to supply a
minimum of 20 per cent of the entries.

4.4   Re-heat facilities are to be on hand, together with
a good supply of hot drinks.

5   Guidelines for Minimum Water Temperatures

5.1   Organisers, in conjunction with their race direc-
tors and medical officer, should give careful consideration to using an alternative venue, or reducing the
distances when the water/air temperature falls below
that which is considered safe.

5.2   The water temperature should be taken from a
point in the middle of the course at a depth of 50cm,
within one hour of the start, and be announced to
competitors at least 15 minutes prior to the start of the
competition.

5.3   The recommended minimum temperature at
which wetsuits should be optional is 14°C (57°F).

5.4   At temperatures of less than 14°C (57°F) the
wearing of wetsuits should be recommended and the
following maximum distances be considered: 13°C
(55°F) 2km; 12°C (54°F) 1km; 11°C (52°F) 500m.

5.5   At temperatures of less than 11°C (52°F) it is
recommended that no open-water swimming takes
place.

5.6   The above guidelines are based on water temperatures alone and assume that the wind-chill factor is
negligible.

5.7   Wherever practical, the ratio of the sections
should be maintained when the swimming distance is
shortened.

6   Cycling

6.1   Every competitor must ensure that their machine
is in a safe and roadworthy condition. In particular, the
machine must be fitted with two independent braking
systems in good working order, with brake levers

securely fastened to the handlebars in such a position
as to enable the rider to apply the brakes while
maintaining a normal riding position. If the machine is
equipped with a fixed wheel with a locking device
properly fitted, then the rear brake may be dispensed
with. Tyres shall be in good condition, and tubular
tyres must be securely fitted to the wheels by a
suitable means of adhesion.

6.2   The use of recumbent machines, protective
shields, wind-breaks, bodywork, or other substantial
means of reducing wind resistance on machines is
prohibited.

6.3   Low-profile machines are permitted, but disc
wheels may only be used on the rear of the machine.

6.4   Prior to the start of the event, each competitor will
either provide the organiser with a signed certificate of
roadworthiness of the machine (in which case spot
checks may be carried out) or submit the machine for
inspection by a machine examiner. Details of which
procedure is to be followed must be included with the
race information.

7   Safety Helmets

7.1   Safety helmets of an approved pattern for road
racing must be worn by competitors at all times during
the cycling section of the event.

8   Assistance

8.1   During the event, competitors are individually
responsible for the repair of their machines. Any
assistance received, other than that provided by the
organisers, will result in disqualification.

8.2   No individual support by vehicle, bicycle, or on
foot is permitted except as provided by the organisers.

9   Numbers

9.1   Competitors must wear the race numbers provided by the organisers throughout the cycling section
of the event, in such a way that they are clearly visible
from behind and/or from the side (left or right as
indicated in the race brief).

10   Completing The Course

10.1   Any part of the course may be covered on foot,
but on these occasions the competitors must carry or
push their own machines.

11   Rules of the Road

11.1   All competitors must follow the normal rules of
the road, obey all traffic signals, and must follow any
directions given by the police, race marshals or
officers. Any infringement of the law and subsequent

legal action is the sole responsibility of the competitor.

12 Pacing/Drafting

12.1 Competitors shall on no account take pace from another cyclist or from a vehicle. The riders must ride alone, singly and not two abreast except for the purposes of overtaking, and must ride no closer than five metres from a rider in front.

12.2 While overtaking another competitor, a rider must pass as widely and as quickly as possible. On no account must there be racing side by side on the course, and as soon as the front wheels are side by side, the overtaken rider must drop back a minimum of five metres behind.

12.3 The onus of dropping back is on the rider being overtaken.

12.4 The five-metre rule is a minimum distance which may be increased at the discretion of the organiser. Details of any increase shall be provided in the race brief.

13 Running

13.1 No form of locomotion other than running or walking is permitted.

13.2 No individual support vehicles, cyclists, or escort runners are allowed.

13.3 All competitors must wear a shirt, vest or trisuit, shorts, etc, and have their issued race number securely fixed and clearly visible from the front, at all times.

13.4 Competitors must follow the directions an instructions of all race officials.

14 Other General Rules

14.1 Competitors are reminded that this is an indi vidual endurance event, and that any team-wor which provides an advantage over other competitor is expressly forbidden.

14.2 Medical personnel have the absolute authori to remove a competitor from the race, who, in the opinion is physically incapable of continuing withou sustaining physical damage or loss of life.

14.3 Any competitor bringing the sport into disrepu is liable to immediate disqualification from the even and possible loss of membership.

14.4 It is the responsibility of all competitors t navigate the prescribed course.

14.5 It is the responsibility of all competitors to repo to the race director, as soon as practicable, an violations of these rules.

14.6 To qualify for the team award in BTA Nation Championships all members must be full members c the same BTA-affiliated club.

14.7 In the running and cycling disciplines, a competitors must wear clothing conforming to recoc nised trisuit patterns or alternatively as acceptable b other authoritative bodies for those competitiv events, when participated in as dedicated activities.

Glossary

Aerobic Training or exercise for which the lungs can supply sufficient oxygen; endurance type training.

Anaerobic Training when insufficient oxygen is supplied.

Anaerobic Threshold The point at which the body can no longer supply enough oxygen for the effort expended. The body goes into oxygen debt at this point.

Asymmetric Uneven (of the body).

Back-To-Back Training Training in one sport or discipline followed immediately by training in another sport or discipline.

Ballistic Recovery Wide recovery of the arms during frontcrawl swimming.

Bilateral Breathing to both sides of the body during swimming.

Crosstraining The effects of training in one sport on performance in another sport or discipline.

Drafting Swimming or cycling (occasionally running) behind another competitor to take advantage of slipstreaming.

Endurance The ability to keep on exerting force against a resistance; cardiovascular endurance relates to the whole body.

Extension The opening of a joint, the opposite of flexion.

Fartlek A Swedish term meaning 'speed-play'. A training session involving either structured or unstructured variations of pace.

Flexibility The quality of large movements at a joint, also called mobility.

Glycogen The basic energy source stored in the muscles (also in the liver).

Hydration (Rehydration) Building up the body's water stores. Rebuilding of the water stores should start immediately after a race or training session.

Hypothermia Loss of heat at the vital core of the body.

Inertia Resistance to movement.

Lactic Acid By-product of anaerobic exercise; muscles cannot contract while it is present.

Overdistance Training Training used to lay the foundations of aerobic fitness; longer than race distances covered at a comfortable pace.

Oxygen Debt The state of the body after anaerobic exercise; it is the amount of oxygen needed to return the body to normal.

Glossary

Physiology   The study of how the body works.

Plantarflexion   Pointing and stretching out of the feet and toes.

Respiration   The process of transporting oxygen into the lungs, then into the tissues, and the removal of carbon dioxide.

Strength   The ability to exert force against a resistance.

Tapering   The period immediately before a competition when the intensity and amount of training is reduced.

Technique   The correct technical movements of swimming, cycling and running.

Training   The whole wide range of organised preparation for performance in triathlon.

VO$_2$ Max (Maximum Oxygen Uptake)   The maximum amount of oxygen that can be delivered to the muscles during intense exericise.

Warm-Down   Gentle movements after exercise which speed recovery.

Warm-Up   The initial exercises taken to prepare the body for strenuous activity.

Useful Addresses

The following is a selective list of local triathlon clubs and contacts:

Bath Amphibians
Leon Smith
Dept of Biochemistry
University of Bath
BA2 7AY

Bedford Harriers
Chris Proud
1 Merlin Gardens
Brickhill
Bedford MK41 7HL

Birmingham Triathlon Club
Nick Price
5 Barnt Green Road
Rednal
Birmingham B45 8ND

Cambridge Triathlon Club
Bill Stewart
10 Woodcock Close
Impington
Cambridgeshire

Club 3 Triathletes
L.K. Whittle
17 The Oaks
Burrage Road
London SE18 7JS

Derbyshire Triathlon Club
Keith Aitken
One Ash Grail
Weston Road
Weston-on-Trent
Derbyshire

Durham Triathlon Club
Stephanie Varty
2 Ford Terrace
Chilton
Co. Durham DL17 0JG

East London Triathletes
Pauline Merritt
2 Stock Street
Plaistow
London N13

Fylde Coast Triathlon Club
Ian Garrod
69 Stadium Avenue
Blackpool
Lancashire FY4 3QA

Ipswich Triathlon Club
Anne Gould
6 Kitchener Road
Ipswich
Suffolk

Jersey Triathlon Club
Josephine Lakeman
11 Le Douettin
Gorey
Jersey

Leicester Triathlon Club
Dave Bellingham
86 Dannett Street
Leicester

Liverpool Triathlon Club
Pat Jarman
22 Barrington Road
Liverpool L15 3HP

Manchester Triathlon Club
John Moore
27 Green Walk
Gatley
Stockport
Cheshire SK8 4BN

Useful Addresses

Mersey Tri
K.J. Westall
62 Balls Road
Birkenhead
Merseyside L43 1US

Metro Rochdale
K. Thompson
5 Moordale Avenue
Oldham
Lancashire OL4 2JP

Milton Keynes Triad
Ray Sutton
139 Arncliffe Drive
Heelands
Milton Keynes MK13 7LF

Norwich Triathletes
Steven Elvin
31 Gamewell Close
Norwich NR1 2RP

Oxford Triathletes
Mike van Oudtshoorn
41 Park Town
Oxford OX2 6SL

Portsmouth Victoria Triathlon Club
Douglas Scobie
45 Horsea Road
Hilsea
Portsmouth PO2 9SP

Sheffield Triathlon Club
Ken Simons
265 Stannington Road
Sheffield S6 5ET

Southampton Triathlon Club
Alison J. Schaab
371c Millbrook Road
Southampton
Hampshire

Thames Turbo Triathlon Club
Dave Jefferies
85 Brookside Avenue
Ashford
Middlesex TW15 3LZ

Thames Valley Triathletes
D. Bowley
30 Stone Street
Reading
Berkshire RG3 1HU

Total Fitness Triathlon Club
T. Gunning
30 Morley Street
Swindon
Wiltshire SN1 1SG

Triathletes London
Will Watson
79 Grosvenor Road
London N10 2DU

Triathletes Swansea
H. Jones
Willow Bank Cottage
Sandy Lane
Parkmill
Swansea SA3 2ER

Tyne Triathlon Club
David Stitt
24 Sheridan Green
Rickleton Village
Washington
Tyne and Wear

York Triathlon Club
Sandy Gott
20 Marlborough Drive
Tadcaster
North Yorkshire

OTHER ADDRESSES

Le Coq Sportif (UK) Ltd
Manor Lane
Holmes Chapel
Crewe
Cheshire CW4 8BB

Terrapin Wetsuits
19 Maple Way
Earl Shilton
Leicester LE4 7HW

Triathlete Magazine
11 Well Lane
East Sheen
London SW14 7AE

Index

Index

Other Titles in The Skills of the Game Series

◆	American Football	Les Wilson
◆	Badminton	Peter Roper
◆	Basketball	Paul Stimpson
◆	Canoeing	Neil Shave
	Cross-Country Skiing	Paddy Field & Tim Walker
◆	Crown Green Bowls	Harry Barratt
◆	Endurance Running	Norman Brook
◆	Fitness for Sport	Rex Hazeldine
◆	Golf	John Stirling
◆	Hockey	John Cadman
◆	Judo	Tony Reay
	Jumping	Malcolm Arnold
◆	Karate	Vic Charles
	Orienteering	Carol McNeill
	Rhythmic Gymnastics	Jenny Bott
◆	Rugby Union	Barrie Corless
◆	Skiing	John Shedden
◆	Skills of Cricket, The	Keith Andrew
◆	Sprinting and Hurdling	Peter Warden
◆	Squash	Ian McKenzie
◆	Swimming	John Verrier
◆	Table Tennis	Gordon Steggal
◆	Tennis	Charles Applewhaite & Bill Moss
	Throwing	Max Jones
◆	Volleyball	Keith Nichols
	Water Skiing	John West
◆	Windsurfing	Ben Oakley

◆ Also available in paperback

Further details of titles available or in preparation can be obtained from the publishers.